No More Clueless Sex

Also by Dr. Gail Elizabeth Wyatt

Stolen Women: Reclaiming Our Sexuality,
Taking Back Our Lives

No More Clueless Sex

10 Secrets to a Sex Life That Works for Both of You

DR. GAIL WYATT
DR. LEWIS WYATT

WILEY

John Wiley & Sons, Inc.

Published by John Wiley & Sons, Inc., Hoboken, New Jersey
Published simultaneously in Canada

Design and production by Navta Associates, Inc.

For general information about our other products and services, please contact our Customer Care Department within the United States at (800) 762-2974, outside the United States at (317) 572-3993 or fax (317) 572-4002.

Wiley also publishes its books in a variety of electronic formats. Some content that appears in print may not be available in electronic books. For more information about Wiley products, visit our web site at www.wiley.com.

Library of Congress Cataloging-in-Publication Data:

Wyatt, Gail Elizabeth.
    No more clueless sex : 10 secrets to a sex life that works for both of you / Gail Wyatt, Lewis Wyatt.
        p.   cm.
Includes bibliographical references and index.
    ISBN 0-471-19485-9
1. Sex instruction. 2. Sex. I. Wyatt, Lewis. II. Title.
    HQ31.W965 2003
    613.9'6—dc22

                                                                    2003016088

Printed in the United States of America

10 9 8 7 6 5 4 3 2 1

We dedicate this book to

God for allowing us to grow up and wise together;

All those people before us who dreamed of the lives
that we live;

Our parents, Lewis Sr., Ruby, Naomi, and Ulysses, who
taught us how to make our dreams a reality;

Lance and Denise, Lacey, Darren and Lauren,
whose vision will carry us; and Kamile and the
rest who will live our dreams;

Michael, in loving memory.

CONTENTS

ACKNOWLEDGMENTS

We deeply appreciate the openness and honesty of the many adolescents and adults who were interviewed for this book and who allowed us to tell their stories. Their names and other identifying information were changed to protect their privacy. Their stories represent the problems that most people face when they search to have a sex life that is satisfying and relationships that are even better.

Getting this message across required that we find the right publisher and an editor who could understand our mission. We are thankful to Madelyn Morel of Lowenstein-Morel Associates for representing us. We appreciate the highly professional staff of John Wiley & Sons who worked tirelessly to produce this beautiful book. We thank Kitt Allan for her support and Lisa Considine for the editorial expertise needed for the final phases. Most of all, we thank Carole Hall for her gentle strength, expertise, wisdom, and passion for our work. Her vision for what this book could be helped us to more clearly focus and write until what we intended to say was said.

So many people worked behind the scenes to research and prepare each chapter. Thanks to Nicole Presley-Green, Marie Vafors, Elizabeth Robles, Michael Marshall, and Dr. John Williams for their invaluable help. Marc Pincus worked to meet every deadline and helped to finish the manuscript. Lynne Olsen's expert artistry beautifully illustrated what only God could create.

This was not an easy project because so much of life still required our attention while we wrote. We appreciate the support of Couples, an organization that explores relationships. Being around friends who also value marriage has helped us to preserve the almost forty years that we have shared. Gloria Powell and Walter Bracklemans challenged us to reinvent ourselves and rediscover what we love and respect about each other.

We thank our family for being so patient and loving over the years that it took to write this book. We've shared both joys and sorrows with them, but with their encouragement, we kept going. We are stronger because we didn't give up.

Finally, we thank you for having the courage to read this book. We hope that it challenges you to learn more and to think differently about sex. There should be no secrets about an experience as potentially beautiful and risky as sex. The last thing you want to be is clueless.

A Letter from the Wyatts

Dear Reader,

A few years ago during the twenty-six-city national book tour for *Stolen Women: Reclaiming Our Sexuality, Taking Back Our Lives,* the idea for this book was born. Everywhere we went, audiences asked for more information about sex and relationships. So many women wanted to know how to make decisions about whom to have sex with, when to have sex, and what kind of sex would work for them. Book signings often lasted many hours with audiences asking questions about how their bodies work sexually and how to avoid painful relationships.

Many people shared their own stories with us. We used some of them in this book. The stories told us that most people were having sex and relationships without a clue as to what was best for them.

Some people in our audiences were more concerned about their loved ones than themselves. They wanted advice on how to help others avoid mistakes that they had made. Most memorable were men who brought their daughters to signings and workshops intent on teaching them sexual health to avoid pregnancies, sexually transmitted diseases, and AIDS. Mothers also brought their sons to discussions to help them understand the importance of not using their sexual performance to define who they are.

Although many in our audiences initially came to support others, each person left taking something away for themselves, as well.

We expect this book will take your sexual knowledge to a new level, no matter who you are. We mainly address sexually active women since female sexuality is our special area of research and medical practice. But men *and* women can benefit from our ideas and most of the recommendations, too. We welcome all readers to share our knowledge. We wrote this book in part so that you, and perhaps your children, too, can tell a different story one day soon.

You are about to learn more than you ever knew about your body, your sexual partner or partners, your needs and fears, your expectations and assumptions, and your untapped sexual potential.

We are so glad you joined us today. This is going to be exciting!

Sincerely,
The Wyatts
Beverly Hills, California

Introduction

For almost thirty years, people have come to us for help with managing and enhancing their sex lives and relationships. As a result, we have spent thousands of hours guiding smart, sensitive people toward the inner harmony and erotic excitement of a sex life that works.

We provide sex therapy training for adults of all ages, for couples and singles, and for adolescents and families. As a clinical psychologist, sex therapist, and sex researcher with training in human sexuality, and an obstetrician-gynecologist with training in sex therapy, we help people solve every kind of sex challenge.

Most people have concerns and dreams, problems and challenges that are a lot like yours or someone you know. For example:

- Sharon, a thirty-something sales manager, came to us for advice on what to do if she ever met her soul mate.

She was still looking, sure she would be physically attracted to and sexually excited by him. So she wanted to be prepared to respond. More to the point, she asked us how to turn him on, too.

- Then there was Larry, a bonds salesman in sexual overdrive. The last thing he wanted was a permanent relationship. For him the payoff for sex was more sex. So he wanted casual, mutually consenting relationships only. But he felt he couldn't be frank about his intentions. He asked how he could find partners and be honest. We knew right away it would take more than conscious resolve for him to change.

- Ben and June, young married professionals, were barely speaking anymore when we met them. June's silence had left Ben clueless about how to improve his sexual performance. Once they had torrid sex almost every night. Now they were dueling. Ben wondered what had gone wrong.

- Teenage Corrine was bursting to have a boyfriend and went overboard on the Internet. When we met her, she felt too embarrassed to tell her mother she'd almost been raped. She had learned her lesson and escaped tragedy, but the memory threatened to sentence her to years of guilt.

- Cynthia, a single executive, had recovered from several breakups and vowed to satisfy her own sexual needs. She came to us for help to figure out how to do it.

This book sums up thousands of hours of listening carefully to stories like these. (For ease of reading, we used third-person narrative, even though only one of us had primary contact with each patient or interview.) Between our practices, we've seen almost every sex and relationship problem you can imagine, and probably some you couldn't make up.

What you will learn from Sharon, Larry, Ben and June, Corrine, Cynthia, and a host of others is that improving your sex life and relationship is an entirely realistic goal no matter who you are.

Here is the key clue to remember: All successful major breakthroughs in sexual pleasure and relationships begin with self-awareness. With sufficient self-knowledge and an understanding of what sex is about, you can unblock obstacles to your pleasure—without risking emotional or physical health—and rescue any relationship worth saving.

Focusing on Patterns of Clueless Sex

By definition, clueless sex is sexual activity in the absence of informed self-awareness. Clueless sex holds you hostage to misinformation, anxious missteps, and the control of partners whose interests oppose yours.

As a a result, you will repeat your cluelessness when it comes to sex and your sex life will settle into one or more of the following patterns:

1. **Clueless assumptions.** Most people are in the dark about how their bodies work before, during, and after sex. Not remarkably, a little more knowledge about the body improves sex almost immediately. We encourage you to take this chance to learn. Many other books explain the mechanics of sex, and we recommend that you read them, too, especially if you aren't very experienced. But this book is different. It's about knowing what turns you on and other secrets that will make you a sexually smarter lover.

2. **Clueless quick sex, or "quickies."** This pattern is almost an epidemic in our fast-food, fast-paced modern world. But as you will see, quick sex doesn't lead to better sex. In

a relationship, quickies may get quicker, but never sweeter. We'll introduce you to the secret alternative.

3. **Clueless lies.** Faking pleasure becomes addictive and distorts your sexuality if you let it. Learn the secret of good social-sexual protocol.

4. **Clueless use of high-tech sex.** Valuable options like vibrators, videos, phone sex, and the Internet get mixed reviews for sexual health and are often hazards to the lonely, isolated user. Learn the techniques of successful high-tech users.

5. **Clueless about the body's potential.** Many relationships flounder because people suffer in silence with their inability to get an erection, experience an orgasm, or even feel much desire for sex. Disabilities also fall into this category, but fear of sex is usually unnecessary, even counterproductive.

6. **Clueless use of drugs.** From not knowing the side effects of birth control pills on your sex drive to ignorance about the influence of alcohol on sexual performance, this may be the most widespread area of clueless sex in our society.

7. **Clueless pain.** People who believe they need to be hurt, suffer, or inflict pain in order to experience sexual pleasure are serious about the games they play.

8. **Clueless victimization.** People who are vulnerable and needy for love and sex tend to attract sexual predators. The irony is that the predators are often men and women in high places, trained for careers that reward them for their aggressive style.

9. **Clueless reactions to grief and stress.** People slip into impulsive sexual liaisons for comfort, often with unintended long-term consequences.

10. **Clueless obsessions and commitments.** Often the result of mental illness, these can just as easily be an expression of lust or well-intentioned but uninformed choices.

Self-Test

Are you wondering where you fit in this picture? Actually, it's wise for you to know. Finding out what impedes your sex life and relationships is what this book is all about. We encourage you to take this self-test. It will provide crucial clues.

1. Has sex disappointed you recently?   Yes   No

2. Do you wonder why you expect so much   Yes   No
   from sex in the first place?

3. Do you worry that you might not be ready   Yes   No
   for what you're getting into sexually?

4. Do you frequently just want a date, when   Yes   No
   your partner wants a whole lot more? Or
   want love, when your partner wants sex?
   Or sex, when your partner wants a
   relationship?

5. Does having sex feel like running a   Yes   No
   marathon? Do you ever wish it would just
   end?

6. Do you and your partner compete to see   Yes   No
   who'll finish first?

7. Do you have "recipe sex"? When you're in   Yes   No
   bed, can you close your eyes and know
   what your partner is going to do next?

8. Did you ever have sex so your partner   Yes   No
   wouldn't leave you?

9. Do you frequently pretend to enjoy sex?   Yes   No
    Do you fake orgasms?

10. Have you recently lied to your partner in   Yes   No
    bed?

11. Do you or your partner need drugs,   Yes   No
    alcohol, the Internet, or videos to make
    sex easier or more exciting?

12. Do you or your partner ever have problems   Yes   No
    becoming excited enough to have sex?

13. Does sex hurt?   Yes   No

14. Do you or your partner have a medical or   Yes   No
    physical condition that makes sex difficult?

15. Is sex something you try to avoid?   Yes   No

16. Do you think your partner might need to   Yes   No
    hurt, control, or take advantage of you to
    make sex more exciting?

17. Do you enjoy being hurt, controlled, or   Yes   No
    taken advantage of?

18. Has it ever proven hard for you to see   Yes   No
    problems in your relationships soon enough
    to protect yourself from being hurt?

19. Would a partner need to leave you before   Yes   No
    you left, even if both of you knew the
    relationship wasn't working?

20. Do you have to struggle to protect yourself Yes   No
    from people who want to use you sexually?

21. Are you afraid or reluctant to talk to   Yes   No
    anyone about any aspect of your sex life?

22. Are you ashamed or embarrassed about   Yes   No
    any part of your sex life?

23. Do you know how high-tech sex could   Yes   No
    enhance or destroy your relationship?

How many *Yes* answers did you come up with? Each indi-
cates two things. One is how experienced in sex you are. The
other is the extent to which your sex life could be enriched by
reading on.

Let's be very clear about this up front. Sex may be working fine for your partner. It may even feel good enough to you.
But every *Yes* you marked is clear testimony that it could be
better, and so could your relationships that involve sex. Like
millions of other people, you're showing signs of being experienced in sex but clueless in love.

To find a way past anger, boredom, frustration, or physical and emotional pain in your love life, you've got to continue
to confront the facts, as hard as they are to accept. Professional
help may be necessary, as we will sometimes indicate. But as
long as you realize that making no move to change, heal, or let
go of the status quo is a clueless way to live and love, we are
delighted you have given us a chance to help.

We can't guarantee that you will find a life-partner or overcome all the obstacles and insecurities that keep people wondering about love. But we do promise to teach you how to
evaluate a potential or current partner for sexual compatibility,
values, maturity, and ability to care about someone other than
themselves.

You'll also learn how to tell where your relationship is
going sexually, what to expect in bed if you stay together, and
why good sex should not change your mind about leaving a bad
relationship. If you are thinking about starting a relationship,
we'll show you how to find out what kind of sex you are going
to be having.

"Exactly what did you have in mind?" just might become
one of your favorite, frequently asked questions.

You may be shy or reluctant to talk about sex now, but it's essential to know how to have conversations about sex. Hint: They should not take place in any room where sex will take place. For a sexual strategy discussion, you should have on all of your clothes in a location where you can leave on your own. We'll prepare you to talk comfortably about everything you want your partner to know, from where to turn you on to your preferred methods of protection from both sexually transmitted diseases and pregnancy.

Learning Better Sexual Strategies

You need to learn to control sex so it doesn't control you. Basically, as you will see throughout this book, control comes from understanding how to think about sex in ways that improve rather than damage relationships. We advise our patients to:

1. Check your sexual history.
2. Learn what attracts you sexually.
3. Understand your sexual scripts.
4. Evaluate what you should change or let go.

Everyone has a sexual history. Think for a minute about how your potential sexual partner's history might affect you and how your history might affect your partner. Even if you have never had sexual intercourse, you have a sexual history that requires your self-awareness. Some people have a history of delaying sexual pleasure and ignoring sexual feelings; for others, it's a matter of knowing only how to please themselves.

We want you to gain the confidence to be yourself, whatever your type and level of sexual experience may be. If your expectations of sex in a relationship are misinformed or distorted, you may have a lot to unlearn. Perhaps you'll need to change your perceptions and increase your knowledge. But there will never be a better time to begin than now.

The past not only influences your deepest feelings about sex, but also affects whom you are attracted to and what you do when you are together. It inevitably shapes your decisions about whom to be with and how you'll act. It's not easy to find and attract a viable sexual partner. But it's sometimes just as hard to know whom to avoid. Some people have deep-seated sexual problems. These individuals don't need to be with anyone at all. They are incapable of a normal, healthy relationship on any terms. Still others do not want permanent relationships and hesitate to be honest about it. These people may feel guilty about misleading you, but they do it anyway. It's tempting to expect more from them emotionally than they are willing to give, even though you are bound to be hurt.

If the people you attract and the relationships you develop are making you uneasy or uncomfortable physically or emotionally, it's probably because you are struggling with memories or physical problems that you need to confront.

When it comes to sex, your job is to know yourself first, then to know your partner. Some people have never experienced sexual desire. Others want sex constantly, or every time they see an attractive person. By striving to understand the implications of your own history, you can learn new skills and choose potential partners who actually appreciate your strengths without taking advantage of your vulnerability. Your ability to become your own best friend is basic to this process. We want you to cherish that ability in yourself.

We'll help you understand why some of your routines aren't working. People are creatures of habit. Repeated often enough, sexual habits have a way of becoming scripts, imprinting on your brain what to do and how to feel. Scripts simplify sex when you don't want to think about what you are doing but feel you must comply. However, there are several potential problems with relying totally on one script all the time.

The most important problem is that sticking with an outdated script takes the fun and adventure out of sex. It's like taking the same road to work day after day. After a while you can practically get there with your eyes closed. You may also end up dissociating or separating your thoughts from your feelings. That's okay if you're driving a car, but not okay if you care about your partner and want that person to care about you.

Scripts can wear out. Sometimes, without realizing it, you might not be getting the skills you need for your relationship from the script you're using. As time goes by, your priorities as well as your body changes. Grief and conflicting commitments can turn your world upside down. It only makes sense that you need to know how to devise new scripts, even in old relationships. Sexual scripts do *not* age like wine. One of the most important skills you will be learning in this book is the art of creating a new script for every relationship and major life change, and, who knows, perhaps for every encounter.

Controlling your script is essential to a sex life that works for you. But knowing and enhancing your partner's script is equally important in a relationship you want to work. When two people take the time to create and exchange scripts, they're much more likely to end up satisfying each other's wants and needs, doing what's best time after time.

We'll also point out if your script leads to relationships or behavior you need to change or let go. Sexiness is powerful. It may surprise you to learn that your sexual behavior is sometimes the only part of you that people find interesting. People who consciously use sex to get love, prizes, attention, fame, and glory assume that one of these days, someone will be interested in who they really are. That is not necessarily true. We'll show you why your actions may be attracting partners for only sex, and nothing more. We candidly discuss almost all the sexual extremes that leave vulnerable people dangerously exposed. We believe that you can learn from their experiences and avoid blindly jeopardizing your own life and happiness.

Even if you are not clueless about extreme sexual risks, you are bound to know someone else who is. What you learn here may be a lifesaver you can pass on to someone you love and want to protect.

Affirmation

Tomorrow when you take that morning stretch, we want you to open this book to this page and recite this affirmation:

> **My gift is everything that I am. I have the capacity for love, passion, and a belief in God. I have the strength and the intelligence to stand up for what I believe in. I will share my gift only with those who earn my love, honesty, trust, and respect. But I will *only* share. My gift belongs to God and me. I will not give my gift away.**

Let's get busy developing your gift. If you have the time or the opportunity to have sex while you are learning to think more clearly about it, that's fine. If you don't, that's probably even better. You can intensify your commitment to concentrate on yourself, what you want from sex, and what you expect from a partner in the future. A period of limited sexual abstinence will enable you to appreciate your sexuality even more.

Until I discover who I am
and who you are
I will be clueless.

—Lewis and Gail Wyatt

1

Clueless Assumptions

Secret #1: Your brain is the sexiest part of your body.

Most people are clueless about how their bodies work during sex. However, if you watch television or videos, go to the movies, or listen to the lyrics of any love song, you might get the impression that love leads straight to an erect penis or a wet vagina.

Thinking what happens between your legs somehow determines your love life is just one of dozens of false assumptions that people carry around about sex. It might surprise you to know how you are turned on, how you decide what feels good, and how your body really responds sexually.

This chapter looks at several of the most common false assumptions we encounter in conversations with people. We've found that the quickest path to improving a person's relationship as well as sexual future is to examine his or her assumptions about how sex works. It's a great shortcut to attitude changes and an instant reality check. There's no guess-work, and only a few background questions are required. In a short period of time, people start feeling better about them-selves and their partners. And when that happens, they become more confident that they can achieve their goals for better sex.

Self Test

1.	If it feels good to you, it is good for you.	True	False
2.	It's never as good as the first time.	True	False
3.	Unless thunder roars and lightning strikes, it isn't good sex.	True	False
4.	Unless your partner has an orgasm, sex wasn't good.	True	False
5.	Sex should last all night.	True	False
6.	Size doesn't matter.	True	False
7.	You can't get pregnant unless he comes inside you.	True	False
8.	He-men, studs, and rappers can't be gay.	True	False
9.	Love conquers all.		
10.	It is easier to make love to the body when you've made love to the mind.	True	False

These assumptions can lead you to expect that your sex life should meet expectations that it can't. In reality, only number 10 is true. Making love to someone begins in the head and not with the body.

Sam and Ann's Strange Attraction

Our patient Sam was certainly surprised and relieved to find out he was wrong about what turned him on. When Sam was a little boy, there was nothing that pleased him more than to come home from school and smell the aroma of freshly baked bread, an apple pie, or dinner coming from his mother's kitchen. Sam, an only child from Austin, Texas, left all of those memories for college in the Northeast and a prestigious job as a young attorney in an up-and-coming Washington, D. C., law firm.

One night Sam and his colleagues were invited to Ann's apartment for a working dinner. Sam arrived rather annoyed that they were wasting time eating when they should have been working, but his mood changed when Ann opened the door. From her kitchen came those very same aromas that he remembered from long ago and Sam got an erection! Embarrassed, he covered himself with his briefcase and immediately sat down.

He came to therapy for advice because he feared that he was becoming sexually aroused by food. We assured him that his fond memories of food evoked a sensuous response that, as an adult, he associated with sexual arousal. He also associated those aromas with the love, warmth, and nurturance that he experienced growing up. Most likely, he would be sexually attracted to a person who could cook. A year later, he sent us an announcement of his wedding to Ann and a note that she had "won him through his stomach."

Actually, she had won him through his brain.

What Turns You On?

If your body and your brain had a contest to see which one is the most important when it comes to sexual attraction, your brain would win. In fact, your brain is the center of all sexual pleasure. It receives and stores all sexual experiences throughout your life and sends signals to your body to behave in a sexual way. Your brain and body communicate. The signals received by your brain are based on what you see, hear, taste, smell, and feel. For Sam, the aromas of home-cooked food were associated with positive memories of loving relationships and happy times.

Signals to the brain are also shaped by your past sexual experiences, expectations, fantasies, and values. Your brain reacts to positive signals by sending a message to the body resulting in sexual arousal. Negative signals turn you off.

THE SEXUAL FUNCTIONS OF THE BRAIN

Hypothalamus	Starts the flow of hormones
Pituitary	Stimulates the ovaries and testicles to secrete sex hormones
Amygdala	Is associated with emotions (fear, anger, happiness, and sadness) and the need to socialize with others
Hippocampus	Retains memory of recent events, stores emotions, and increases heart rate
Septal Area	Is associated with pleasurable sensations
Cranial Nerves	Carry signals from the brain to the body and back

Sex is undeniably a total body experience. Even your skin sends signals to the brain. All over your body, areas of sexual pleasure called erogenous zones report to your brain.

It's easy to assume that everyone experiences sexual pleasure the same way; after all, we have the same basic brain and body parts. But this is another one of those common assumptions that stands in the way of developing useful sexual knowledge. In truth, everyone has different areas of pleasure, and it is important, even crucial, for you to find your own. If you can't tell your partner what's going on when he touches you there or in that way, he'll only find out by trial and error. Sometimes this can be a waste of time.

Your brain is busy storing messages based on your experiences, and you are constantly labeling and relabeling what feels good to you and what doesn't. Other people will tell you that you should or should not enjoy being touched in certain places and ways, especially as a child but as an adult, your own experiences may contradict those assumptions. Your parents, religious leaders, friends, or loved ones may try to guide you toward experiences that they enjoy and away from those they don't. But having sex is such a deeply personal emotional and biological experience that they will never know completely what you enjoy.

Likewise your sexual pleasure can be enhanced and shared with a partner, but it is not defined for you by your partner—unless you allow it. Learning what attracts and arouses you sexually is one of the first lessons in life that no one else can fully prepare you for or teach you completely. Since experience is your most reliable teacher, your responsibility to yourself is to seek good experiences and avoid bad ones.

Here's a Clue to Remember

All too often, sex involves the exclusive use of the penis and the vagina. Imagine the fun you could have exploring all over your body for hidden erogenous zones and mapping them. Try it! Mark them on the diagrams on pages 18 and 19. Mark your partner's, too. *Hint:* Feet, skin, and breasts are arousal sites for both men and women.

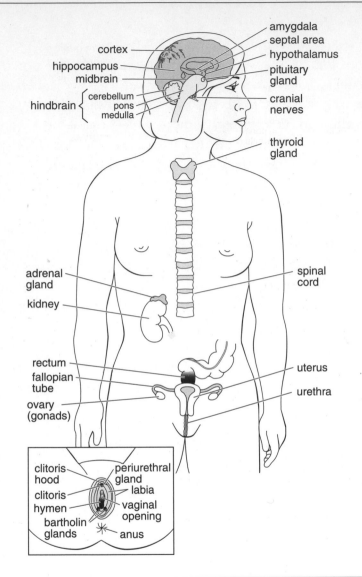

Ovaries	Secrete estrogen, progesterone, and testosterone. Help control menstruation and fertility.
Vagina	Receives and stimulates the penis
Clitoris	Arousal site
"G" Spot	Arousal site

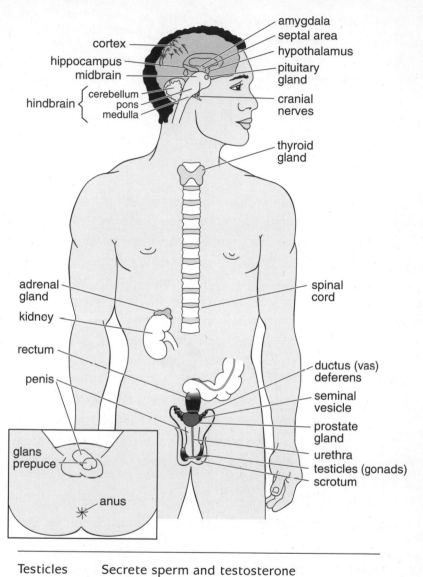

| Testicles | Secrete sperm and testosterone |
| Penis | Penetrates and stimulates the vagina, mouth, and anus. |

How Your Body Says It's Ready

Do you know that the brain gives the body a green light for intercourse, or sexual penetration? Having adequate foreplay, or making out until lubrication occurs, helps the body to be ready for sex. This self-lubricating process takes a little or a lot of time. It also requires a certain level of stimulation of both the brain and the body, such as tender talking, looking at a sexy movie, caressing your own body, or kissing your partner.

When a woman's vagina is wet enough for sex, it will feel moist at the point of entry and there will be less resistance than there would be otherwise when insertion of the penis begins. But getting to this point can be tricky. Some women self-lubricate adequately at the beginning of sex but fail to continue lubricating throughout. Others fail to lubricate until after penetration.

This variation in the individual response is why women and their partners need to keep a store-bought water-based lubricant handy if they're sexually active. Brands such as KY Jelly, Vagisil, Astroglide, and others are available in drugstores everywhere, so there's no excuse for not keeping some with you. Save your Crisco, Vaseline, olive oil, spittle, or hair products for what they were intended and avoid using them as lubricants.

The recommended lubricants for vaginal and anal penetration also help minimize the risk of bruising, tearing, and infection. Have you ever pressed on the brakes in your car when they need to be replaced? You hear scraping and know you are doing damage. Some partners will literally scrape the lining off your sexual organs if you let them and never stop to apologize, much less feel genuine regret for the consequences to you. Don't assume that your partner knows or cares about your needs. Have we made it clear that buying and using a lubricant is up to you?

If you could look at your vagina under a microscope after sexual intercourse, you would find numerous small tears and bruises. If a vagina is not lubricated or has just begun that process or if it becomes dry before intercourse ends, more bruising and tearing occurs, and that can lead to infection. If the bartholin glands at the entrance of the vagina are damaged, they can swell and stop providing lubrication. Sex can become even more painful.

You might find even more tears and bruises after having anal sex, when the penis enters the bottom or ano-rectal canal. The vagina has the ability to self-lubricate and open for the penis to enter, but the anus has a very thin lining that tears easily and opens with more difficulty.

The penis does not lubricate on its own. If there is active thrusting for long periods of time, a man's penis can experience itching, burning, and infection if it is not lubricated sufficiently with body fluids or a store-bought lubricant. These symptoms can lead to physical discomfort and sexual dissatisfaction.

Remember This Crucial Clue

Never forget, any opening in the body that lubricates poorly or dries out before the sexual act ends needs a water-based lubricant. The failure to be lubricated over time can result in damage, infection, swelling, pain, and a desire not to have sex. As a consequence, medical attention and sex therapy may be necessary. As you grow older, you will have to work harder to achieve lubrication naturally. It's going to be increasingly important to have the good sense to buy a drugstore lubricant.

What Characterizes a Sexual Response?

There's more science than romance or mystery involved in the human sexual response. Even though different people respond to entirely different stimuli, it is the specific nature of the response that makes it sexual. The same process (hormones and nerve stimulation) that causes lubrication in the female brings about erection in the male. It is primarily testosterone and nerve stimulation that increases blood flow to the penis, making it firm and erect. Following signals from the brain, this process usually occurs within *seconds*. Similarly, female hormones (estrogen, progesterone, and testosterone) and nerve stimulation cause clitoral erection and vaginal lubrication.

Thus, with the proper amount of stimulation and the right setting, a female:

- Will usually become relaxed and seem less rigid and stiff
- Will feel her nipples and clitoris become erect
- Will breathe deeply and might begin to perspire
- Will feel her vagina get wet
- Might arch her body

Under the same conditions, a male will:

- Get a partial or full erection
- Breathe deeply and perspire
- Try to insert his penis whether his partner is ready or not

Did you notice that last bulleted item? Did you take note of the warp speed with which men get the brain's signal for erection? Did you see the "might's" in the woman's response list? The differences are intriguing. No wonder we hear from so many males who rush hotly ahead through sex and from their unhappy partners who are left wanting more.

Many men literally have to be told that the best way, if not the only way, to find out if a woman is ready for sex is to ask her. Think about it. If you don't tell him, who will? And who pays if you don't?

Helping Him Gauge Your Sexual Response

We recommend that a woman pay more attention to her own sexual response and assume accountability for reporting it to her partner. It may be one of the simplest and most effective changes you can make on your own to bring you closer to the sexual results and understanding you want: Tell your partner you'll signal him when you are ready. He can make his move when you say "go."

Who's Responsible for Your Body When You're Having Sex?

Each individual's view of his or her responsibility for the other depends on too many social, religious, and moral factors to name here. But suffice it to say that this is one area where it's dangerous to assume anything. It may be a matter of life or death.

Do you know your general health history? Get a full physical exam including tests for HIV and sexually transmitted diseases (STDs). Show each other your written results. Make sure you understand what the test results mean. The best way to fully understand your health history is to take your results to a health professional who can tell you what they mean. You may also need to make some decisions about changing what you eat and how you live. It's up to you to do whatever is necessary to protect yourself from outcomes you don't want. We assume doing so involves making a few compromises.

Yet we also know couples who think they don't have time to carefully use condoms or other types of contraception like a diaphragm, suppository, or vaginal ring. Too little time spent using these devices increases the chance of their slipping off or moving out of place. The associated fear of unintended pregnancy, STDs, or HIV/AIDS decreases sexual satisfaction. This is particularly true between strangers who know little about each other's past partners. If neither has been tested for STDs or HIV, or has not seen results from recent testing, the couple is not ready for sex.

In the majority of cases, these couples are amazed when we tell them that putting on a condom can be pleasurable, especially if the woman puts it on her partner. And a man can be very sexy when he puts on his own condom. This thoughtful gesture could mean that he cares enough to protect both of them from any unexpected consequences of sex, or simply that he's realistic about the connection between sex and survival.

What Are Your Assumptions about Orgasms?

Fantasy, consistent touch, or heightened sexual contact may result in your becoming orgasmic, or "coming." An orgasm is a surge of sexual feelings that build in intensity until they peak and subside. At the height of the sexual surge, the penis and the vagina may contract. A stream of fluid, or semen, is ejected from the tip of the penis. A warm fluid may also flow into the vagina. With these feelings comes a release of sexual tension that can also increase from one orgasm to the next. The orgasm afterglow includes pleasant and peaceful emotions that can be very relaxing. Sometimes men confuse a woman's sexual arousal with her orgasm and believe that she has been totally satisfied. Actually, sexual pleasure for her may be just beginning.

Orgasms are very addictive. People who have experienced one are likely to try to experience another. Your attraction to anyone who makes it possible for you to experience an orgasm will become stronger, though you don't necessarily need a partner. You can become orgasmic by yourself, thanks to your brain.

The "G" Spot

- Is known by other names: the spot, the sacred spot, the black pearl, or the sensitive spot

- Is located 2 to $2\frac{1}{2}$ inches on the upper wall from the opening of the vagina

- When stimulated by a penis or a dildo, can make an orgasm more intense

Does What You Did during Puberty or Young Adulthood Matter Anymore?

By now, your body already has quite an impressive sexual base. And it's still developing.

By birth, several important phases of sexual development have already occurred. At about thirty-one weeks before birth, the presence of testosterone, the male hormone, causes a baby to develop a penis, the male sex organ. If testosterone is not present in a sufficient amount, the baby will develop a clitoris and vagina, the female sex organs. Males are also born with testes, the two egg-shaped balls in the scrotum (sac-like bags between the legs) that produce testosterone. Females are born with ovaries that produce estrogen, progesterone, but less testosterone than males produce. These hormones help the body to prepare for sexual activity. The testes will mature to produce sperm in males, tadpole-like cells that fertilize the eggs from female ovaries. The testes and ovaries mature at puberty, which occurs, on average, between the ages of eleven and thirteen. Although the brain still needs time to develop in order for the individual to make decisions about healthy sexual relation-ships, the body is physically ready for sex.

At puberty secondary sex characteristics appear as a result of increased levels of hormones. Secondary sex characteristics make you look physically mature and prepare your body for sex-ual activity and reproduction. For example, in females, the pitu-itary gland, located in the brain, signals the ovaries to release hormones to start monthly periods, develop breasts, widen the hips, narrow the waist, and grow underarm and pubic hair.

Under the influence of testosterone, males also change at puberty. Their shoulders widen; their hips narrow; and their muscles, their penises, and their scrotums increase in size. Facial, chest, and pubic hair begin to grow and the voice deep-ens. Being bombarded with all these sexual and emotional signals is a very intense experience. Masturbation or self-stimulation may relieve some physical tension, but can also add to the emotional intensity.

For some, the process of sexual development takes longer, which can cause a great deal of anxiety, according to these per-sonal recollections:

> I remember puberty. I was thirteen years old when I first saw peach fuzz above Harvey's upper lip. He was already growing a mustache and I wasn't. He was no older, but he was getting attention from girls that I wasn't and leaving me behind. His testosterone was kick-ing in and he would soon have a deeper voice and pre-sumably a larger penis than I would. His body looked more like he was ready for sex than mine did. I began to inspect my upper lip daily, hoping for the day when I would show physical proof that I, too, was growing up.

> When I was in high school, my greatest goal was to be able to wear a straight skirt. Of course, I was in my sec-ond semester when I finally got the courage to wear one

to school. When I walked into homeroom, a boy asked me, "Where are your hips?" It took me another year before I found the courage to wear another skirt like that again.

These are examples of how we struggle to reach the markers in our development that signal to others that we are "grown up." However, depending on how much support you get during that process, what is said about you will be remembered for years.

The most challenging issues most teens face are sexual or have sexual implications:

- When they should become sexually active
- What behaviors are acceptable to the adults who are responsible for their care
- Their acceptability to their peers

All these sexual pressures influence how people handle the physical and emotional intensity of adolescence.

By the late teenage years or young adulthood, emotional development catches up with physical development, which should allow you to make decisions that leave you feeling good about yourself and your relationships. From that point on, the more you know about your sexuality and when and with whom you prefer to have sex, the more carefully you can select relationships important to you. Having sex with the wrong person or in the wrong place or at a certain time in your life will definitely affect your sexual pleasure and how you feel about your ability to control your sex life in the future.

Most men and women in their late teens and early twenties have had sex at least once. How much education you received; your family income; mental health; religious, spiritual, and cultural beliefs about sex; the kinds of traumatic sexual and physical experiences you had; and your use of drugs or alcohol all play a part in how long you wait before becoming sexually active and how you feel about and perform during sex now.

Does Size Matter?

When it comes to sex, one of the greatest challenges is to accept your body as it is. Does that surprise you? This may not be your number one challenge, but it should be in your top ten. A large penis and large breasts are valued in most societies. A small penis and a large vagina are not. But the answer to the question does size matter? is *yes* and *no*.

Size actually matters less in terms of sexual performance than it does in terms of social expectations and status. Women can strengthen their vaginal muscles with Kegel exercises, so that the vagina can accommodate a penis of any size. It's a matter of knowledge and technique. And, likewise, a small penis can be directed toward the clitoris, the "G" spot, and areas of the vagina that are most sensitive to increase sexual pleasure. A large penis will more easily hit the "G" spot and most other parts of the vagina.

How you feel about the size of your genitals and other body parts will influence your self-esteem and the kinds of relationships you seek, but only if you allow your genitals to define who you are as a person. Regardless of the size of your genitals and body parts, it's what you do with them that really counts in your sex life.

Kegel Exercises

By squeezing the pelvic floor muscles when contracting the vagina or stopping your flow of urine in midstream, you can strengthen and control your vagina. These exercises should be done daily. Clench, squeeze, or contract the floor muscles surrounding the vagina for a count of five, relax, and repeat twenty times. Repeat this five to ten times a day.

What about Aging?

Your body is also changing throughout your life, as is your partner's. Accepting those changes is critical to realistic expectations from your sexual performance. The most dramatic change that affects sexual functioning occurs when your hormones begin to decline.

Menopause is the age at which the ovaries no longer produce eggs or secrete estrogen and progesterone. Even though the brain continues to send signals, the body does not respond as it has in the past. A woman, after the age of forty, who has had no period for six months and is not pregnant is considered menopausal. The average age of menopause is 51.3 years of age in the United States. Women then remain postmenopausal for the rest of their lives. Shortly before or during menopause, women may experience pain during sex because of vaginal dryness, a result of having trouble lubricating. Mood changes, hot flashes, night sweats, and insomnia can also affect a woman's interest in sexual activity.

Aging affects men just as it does women. They experience a gradual decline in testosterone after age forty and a rapid decline after age sixty that affect their sex drive. Older men may also experience changes in the firmness of their erections or have more difficulty in achieving erections. The brain is still sending signals, but either the body responds more slowly or it does not respond with the same intensity for sex.

These dramatic changes, like every other aspect of sexual change and growth, will require your patience, understanding, and determination to find new ways to experience sexual pleasure, regardless of the challenges. You need time to know yourself and modify what you want, setting new priorities at each stage of life.

2

Clueless Quickies

Secret #2: When you race to the finish, you don't always win.

If you and your partner always make beautiful, deeply passionate life-affirming love, this book will help keep it that way. But what if your sex life leaves something—or a lot—to be desired? That was our patient Ben's case. He was facing one of the most common sexual relationship problems that results from sticking with one script.

Here's how we met Ben and helped him give his love life a sexual makeover.

Ben's Script: Slam, Bam, Thank You, Ma'am

It is not often that people run to the office of a sex therapist. Everyone wants to seem cool and experienced in sex, even if they aren't. But fear had forced Ben to take desperate measures. This young lawyer literally ran into the office with his tie over his shoulder and breathlessly apologized for being late.

"I'm always in a hurry," he explained. Then he launched into his story about his problem with his wife. "June and I are not enjoying sex anymore. She is not even interested in having sex with me. She says she loves me but needs more. More of what? I just don't get it. I'm really confused and hurt. She used to say that I was an exciting lover, but now she rejects me."

"Hold on, Ben. How have you had sex in the past, even before June?" we asked, beginning to take his history to identify his sexual pattern. "What about the first time?"

"How could I forget?" he said. "I was fourteen, horny, and hooked up. My older brother had a friend who would let me make out with my girlfriend in the backseat of his car. She was nineteen and had an after-school job, so we never had much time. She pretty much showed me what to do. I came quickly. It was unbelievable. When I got my own car, I started having sex in the backseat pretty regularly. I had to be creative because it was so cramped, but it worked out just fine.

"In college it was pretty much the same. I had sex in my car or in the girl's dorm room. I liked it best when the roommate was just down the hall. It was more exciting that way. I graduated and landed a plush job where my boss was not much older than me. She had been married several years but came on to me as soon as I was hired. We had to be discreet and would dash from work at lunch to go to my apartment nearby, have sex, and return to work within the hour. She was something. A real professional at work, but, as she said, 'I'm a slut with skills in the bedroom.'

"Boy, we were taking care of business. Eventually, I dated other girls but nobody was as exciting or willing to please me as my boss was. She wore me out. I was coming between one and two times a day on my Monday through Friday work-sex-work schedule. Pretty soon I was living to go to work, but I wasn't getting much work done. I was thrilled that an older, attractive, married woman was interested in me.

"When my boss's husband was transferred to another state, our affair ended. But, before she left, we had a sex marathon. She and I spent one entire day together in my apartment. We had sex so many times, I lost count. In fact, when she left, I could barely walk. She joked that I was like a prizefighter in the first round of a fight, always finishing early with a TKO.

"I really missed her for a while, but shortly after she left, I met June. I really did not want to have sex as much as I'd had before, but June was just as exciting to me as my former boss and I continued my same pattern of frequent quick sex. I seemed to satisfy June at first so you can see why this change in our sex life has me confused."

The Inside Story: Too Much of a Good Thing

Quickies, the essence of Ben's sexual script, were the only kind of sex he had ever had, so he didn't have a clue how they were limiting his sexual potential. He had never savored long, luscious, gourmet sex with his partners. To the contrary, he thought he was a superior lover until a steady diet of quickies became a problem for his wife.

We hardly know anyone who doesn't like quick sex once in a while. Why? If orgasms are what you want from sex, quickies can get you there without having to waste time. When anxiety heightens arousal, sex can last for less than five minutes, including the orgasm. That's why it's called a quickie. Like fast food, you don't have to wait to get it. It's hot and, if you're really hungry, it's going to taste so good while you're eating it that you may want to keep eating long after you're full. That is, if you've never had a gourmet meal.

Quickies are the classic pattern of boys younger than

eighteen. If you saw the movie *Y Tu Mama, Tambien,* you'll remember the image of teenagers going at it with minutes to spare before catching a plane or being discovered in the back-seat of a car. The quick-sex pattern usually begins during adolescence. By adulthood, it becomes hard to unlearn. Lovers easily become convinced that this exciting and often risky pattern is just what they need all the time. Without learning how to have gourmet sex, which is different each time and is satisfying for both partners, quickies just get quicker, not better. They are also common among partners who are overcontrolling. They tend to love a routine so that they can predict and control every movement during sex. These partners can sometimes be very selfish and intimidating.

Ben was more confused than controlling. He was simply accustomed to being shown what his partner wanted. His past liaisons involved older, more experienced women who gave him direction. He was also used to a fast genital response from himself and his partners. Ben's entire sexual experience involved quick sex. When he met June, a banker, they were physically attracted to one another and fell in love. However, they both held highly demanding jobs. They often had conflicting schedules and did not place a priority on leisurely sex. They were young, healthy, and could be orgasmic within ten minutes, with almost any kind of sexual stimulation. They used their time management skills and reduced their sexual contact to five minutes to make it even more exciting. They expected that it would never take much more time than that to satisfy each other sexually. But June, while initially excited by their passion, expected more from sex.

What June Expected, but Wasn't Telling Ben

The fact that quickies were the only way Ben and June made love became a problem for June. She expected more leisurely, satisfying sex. However, instead of telling Ben specifically that she needed more time, space, intimacy, and creativity in their sex life, June was nonspecific in the way she communicated her concerns and simply rejected all of Ben's sexual advances.

Ben, convinced that their initial interest in quickies was still shared by them both, maintained that they had no problem. He was unaware that June's silent rejection meant that she wanted to change their sexual script, so he continued the pattern that June was no longer interested in. Her frustration turned to stiff anger at his insensitive response.

June needed to communicate her sexual needs more effectively and show Ben what she did and did not like. But anger took over. Her hesitancy about taking more responsibility for their sexual encounters turned into a cold silence. Ironically, Ben would most likely have welcomed her assertiveness because he was used to his partners directing his sexual activity. He probably would have encouraged her to speak openly to him about what she liked and disliked.

Being angry in silence just distances two people from each other, damages the relationship, and reinforces the clueless habit of avoiding difficult topics. Unresolved anger turns sizzling sex into embers.

Intimacy Takes Time

The ultimate reward of sustaining a long-term relationship is the ability to reveal your innermost feelings and thoughts. When you take time to initiate verbal and physical intimacy before and after sex, the payoff is enormous.

Sex is no more than mechanical action if the genitals are the only organs that you use. Kissing your partner twice, touching one breast, being penetrated or penetrating someone, and having an orgasm is really an abbreviated form of intercourse.

R$_x$ for a Healing Conversation about Sex

Step One

Instead of forcing a showdown, we recommend that partners who sincerely want to try to change things for the better set aside uninterrupted time for making up in a private setting.

Use this time to plan your next sexual encounter. You'll need at least an hour for this conversation if you expect to deal with real issues in a leisurely, respectful way. Here's how to begin:

- **Agree on ground rules of communication.** No yelling, physical abuse, intimidation, threats, or walking away should be allowed. If one person becomes upset, reschedule the discussion to a later time. *Warning: If you can't agree on ground rules, or if your safety concerns you, don't continue with this prescription on your own. Seek professional counseling.*

- **Take turns describing what you would like to have happen the next time you have sex.**

- **Take turns describing what needs to change to make it happen.** Try not to be defensive. Try to draw your partner out but be careful not to expect so much that you set yourself up for further disappointment.

- **Acknowledge any needs that seem to be very different between you.**

Step Two

Next, to help you focus on your expectations and attitudes, work through the following questions together, asking each other:

1. **Do we skip foreplay?**

   Do you have the impression that flirting, kissing, hugging, touching each others' breasts or genitals with your hands or mouth, or rubbing your bodies together before sexual intercourse is a waste of time?

2. **Do we get excited because of where we are?**

   Do you become aroused in the backseat of a car, on the kitchen table, in airplane bathrooms, or in an elevator? Does having sex in forbidden places while risking being discovered increase your anxiety and excitement but reduce your feeling of intimacy?

3. **Would a new partner make me more excited?**

   What do you have going for you in your relationship that keeps you together besides sex?

4. **Do we swing rapidly from being passive to frantically ripping off our clothes?**

   Could it be that this drama is getting a little worn? Could you try a variation, like keeping certain items of clothing on? Trading certain items? Stripping while dancing is another way to slow things down and "get things up" at the same time.

5. **Do we use alcohol or drugs to heighten our excitement and increase our willingness to have sex at lightning speed?**

   Have you tried sex without a stimulant? Why not see what it's like? Or try an audio or visual stimulant such as a CD, a radio, or a music video.

6. **Do we expect a great sexual rush?**

   Do you have quick sex to have an orgasm rather than bother with all the parts of sex that take time and effort? Do your thoughts and feelings give way to pure genital pleasure?

Step Three

If you've gotten this far, you're already making progress on your makeover of this relationship. Keep working out a solution.

- **Invite your partner to go to the library or bookstore with you.** Look for pictures of sexual positions that are new to you. (Don't be surprised if some of the books and manuals are very old. People have been experimenting for centuries with methods to make lasting good sex!)

- **For your rendezvous, choose a place that will allow you to spread out.** Avoid being cramped into small places.

- **Increase each other's anticipation of the date** by sending (confidential) e-mail, phone messages, and cards during the day or prior to your getting together. Splurge on buying fluffy new towels and pillows. Make the setting as romantic as you want to feel.

- **When you meet, immediately slow down the pace.** Start by listening to music, talking, or playing games together. Try relaxing in a bubble bath. Scent the water with a fragrance you both like. Caress without making love. Just enjoy being together in this serene way.

- **When you're ready, tell your partner exactly what you want to do** and what positions you want to try, even if both of you have not tried them before.

- **Praise your partner lavishly** for being willing to explore new sexual experiences.

It's like reading CliffsNotes rather than a best-seller or like seeing a preview but never the movie. Like Ben and June, you miss the opportunity to experience emotional bonding on a level other than a brief encounter.

Having sex is one of the most personal acts that humans perform. The level of emotion you can reach depends as much on what you say and do before and after sex as what you do in the midst of it. Whenever you verbally convey to your partner his or her value in your life, you reaffirm to yourself that you have the ability to feel very deeply and tenderly about another person. Your partner needs to know that you appreciate the way he or she feels about you, too.

Is Your Partner Masking a Physical Problem?

Ben and June started practicing leisurely sex and slowed their lovemaking down. It was then that they realized that he was ejaculating too soon to allow June to become orgasmic. Quickies may be a mask for partners, like Ben, who come too soon or ejaculate prematurely. Instead of disclosing that they need to work with you on learning how to prolong intercourse, partners addicted to quickies may either attempt to speed up sex to hide their dysfunction or deny that they have any problems.

But Ben and June were learning how to enjoy sex, enhance their relationship, and work on their emotional bond and intimacy. Ben soon lost his defensiveness. June and Ben came to several sessions together where we taught them how to control Ben's ejaculations. By our last session, he sauntered into the room, on time, tie in place, and with a smile on his face.

The Squeeze Technique

At home, June practiced how to squeeze the glans of Ben's penis with her fingertips, which would lessen his desire to ejaculate. Then they used this technique during intercourse. When Ben felt the urge to "come," he would withdraw his penis. June would apply the squeeze technique. Once the sensation to ejaculate lessened, Ben would reenter June and enjoy intercourse until the urge recurred. If they were ready to stop, he came; if not, June applied the squeeze technique again.

The Withdrawal Technique

Ben also learned to withdraw his penis before the urge to come was too great without using the squeeze technique and to reenter June when the urge subsided.

Are You Masking an Emotional Need?

Why do smart people develop sexual habits that any sex expert would guarantee to fail? Consider Johnette's story. She was the last of five girls in her family. Her sisters were usually praised for their beauty, but Johnette felt ordinary. To compensate for her low self-esteem, she fell into a hip-hop crowd and became

---

Remember This Clue

One sure sign that your partner suspects he might have a problem is if he gets defensive and says, "There's something wrong with you, not me!" or "I'm finished. You'd better hurry up."

---

sexually active at a young age. She grew into adulthood never having had an orgasm, but she was the queen of the quickie in her neighborhood.

While the guys only wanted her for sex, the attention and even notoriety she gained made her feel important and wanted. Her parents learned about her reputation, but instead of attempting to understand what she was gaining by using her body, they sent her to live with relatives. Initially, her aunt and uncle were able to monitor her activities, but when they started to trust her and extend her privileges, her feelings of worthlessness emerged again and she returned to the same old sexual pattern.

Johnette used sex to feel better about herself, using her body to gain love, attention, and acceptance. Once she began to receive counseling to break the cycle of tolerating quick sex, she was able to confront her desperate need to love and respect herself.

Don't be surprised if you do not have a wide range of feelings. Writing them down helps to make the point that you may be better able to identify what makes you sad or mad, but not

R$_x$ for Healing Self-Esteem

- Think about who you are, what you want out of life, and how you can accomplish your goals other than through having sex. Write those goals down and tape them on your bathroom mirror. Read and renew daily your commitment to these goals.

- Keep a daily record of your good and bad feelings and the incidents that provoke them. Make a note of the things that make you smile, hurt your feelings, make you angry or sad, etc.

happy. When you are unhappy for long periods of time, you may increase the chances of looking for partners who can make you happy. The reality is you are responsible for your own happiness and satisfaction. If you accept this responsibility, you may be more likely to find a relationship that works.

As Johnette developed a different perspective about sex and changed her expectations, she began to make different decisions. Her sexual and emotional transformation came together, reflected in the new value she placed on attracting relationships that gave her a better chance for a safe and satisfying sex life.

Partners who want to avoid a committed relationship or spending time with you may prefer quickies. They may be selfish lovers who really don't care if you are orgasmic or not ("I though she was aroused, or she had an orgasm")—but they never ask. They prefer the mechanics of sex and quick orgasm but don't want the opportunity for emotional bonding or intimacy. They have a script and tend to follow it.

Getting Ready to Change

In a relationship, it is important for you to discuss any decision to change your behavior with your partner. Be ready to hear what your partner says, not just what you want to hear.

Once you make your commitment, check in with your partner on a regular basis. You need to know if you and your partner are on the same page in the relationship. Some couples find that weekly discussions are very helpful. In a shaky relationship, it's better to communicate anxious feelings than it is to hold them in. Pacing your sex life and learning how to enjoy your partner is the remedy for a lot of problems that can initially leave you clueless about how to make sex work.

Get a Clue

If a future sexual partner is not your friend, how can you trust them with your body, your feelings, your health, and your life? How can you be trusted, as well?

3

Clueless Lies

Secret #3: You don't have to fake it if your relationship is real.

Remember the scene in the motion picture *When Harry Met Sally* where Meg Ryan faked an orgasm in a restaurant? Her performance was so convincing that it scared men to death. Before that movie scene, many men were unaware that women could pretend to experience sexual ecstasy.

Faking is much easier for women than for men. It's impossible for a man to hide an erect penis during intercourse and the resulting semen. A woman, on the other hand, can have intercourse without her nipples and clitoris becoming erect. And she may or may not ejaculate when she comes. A warm surge of feelings builds and becomes more intense as her body arches, tenses, and relaxes during a real orgasm. But how is anyone else going to know what she's feeling if she only goes through the motions? Besides, while women tend to prefer orgasms during sex, unlike men, they can be sexually satisfied without having one. The fact is that men tend to be orgasm-focused. Many men go as far as equating being good sexual lovers with the ability to give their partners orgasms.

The Sexual-Social Protocol

Faking usually has more to do with manipulating the male ego than anything else. Three out of four women know this. They've either faked an orgasm or greatly exaggerated their sexual pleasure for one reason: it works.

By feigning pleasure, you can accomplish several things simultaneously:

- Create the impression that you and your partner finish or become orgasmic at the same time, an illusion that men find particularly satisfying
- Disguise the fact that you are really not aroused enough by your partner to have an orgasm
- Avoid conflict or hurting your partner's feelings
- Mask not really enjoying sex in a relationship you want to keep

For most women, faking sexual pleasure from time to time is not a big deal, though. It's simply a matter of social protocol.

Think about it for a minute. If a friend invited you to dinner and cooked a truly forgettable meal, you wouldn't call her a lousy cook, would you? No, you would thank her for the evening, especially if you valued your relationship or sensed that her feelings were on the line. Besides, the next time she invited you over for dinner, you could always offer to take her out or to cook the meal yourself.

When it comes to sex, the same protocol can apply. It's

often better to finesse a mediocre or disappointing sexual encounter by saying something gentle but noncommittal.

"I love being with you" will do. Then you are free to clear the slate later and avoid a "next time" by easing out of the relationship or directing it away from sex.

Faking pleasure is not a problem, but going overboard and telling a whopping lie is. You wouldn't lavish compliments on your friend's tasteless, overdone chicken, would you? So why go on and on raving about your partner's performance, implying you're having a wonderful time?

"This was the best sex of my life!" or "You're the best lover I have ever had" is not the smartest thing to say when you haven't been orgasmic or sexually satisfied by any part of the whole experience—unless what you want is more bad sex the next time.

However, our client Anya didn't see it that way.

Anya and Quentin: Faking for Favors

Anya, a beautiful thirty-year-old woman, was a concierge in a trendy, upscale hotel that attracted business travelers from

> **Remember This Important Clue**
>
> A relationship that works for you as well as it does for your partner doesn't depend on either of you being totally honest 100 percent of the time. But it does require a significant level of honesty and a fundamentally caring attitude. Any secrets that you keep or lies that you tell can and will come back to haunt you, so it is obviously in your best interest to be as honest as possible as often as possible.

Fortune 500 companies. Anya made it her business to get the very best for her clients: front-row seats to shows and the best tables in popular exclusive restaurants. She made contacts all over town until she could call almost anywhere at the last minute and get exactly what her clients wanted. She was so successful that she was promoted and began working full time in guest services, which was just what she wanted.

Anya was more than happy to go to dinner with Quentin, an executive guest who was more than thirty years her senior. After many toasts, she helped him back to his room. When Quentin woke up the next morning, he found Anya next to him in bed wearing nothing but his shirt and a smile. She raved about "the best sex she had ever had," which motivated him to see her again. She played hard to get, but essentially, the die was cast.

Quentin was amazed at how easily he could arouse her and how sexy she made him feel. His wife had become less and less interested in sex, although they shared a great life together. He could not get over the fact that he was a better lover with Anya. She moaned and groaned every time Quentin laid a finger on her, apparently having one orgasm after another, even though he often had difficulty getting and maintaining an erection. Feeling trapped, Quentin realized that he had to be careful what he asked for. He was having more sex with Anya than ever in his life, but he valued the quality of his relationship with his wife more.

Anya, on the other hand, had different expectations. She was seeking financial security and social status. Having a real sexual attraction to Quentin or any potential partner was not as important to her as how she was rewarded for acting sexually responsive. That was her script. Some men preferred Anya to partners who demanded sexual prowess or who were not interested in sex at all. Even if these men knew she was faking, they would never say so.

The Inside Story: The Relationship Bargain

While pretense has its place in social-sexual protocol, there is a problem when one partner habitually colludes with the other.

"If you have sex the way I want it and you pretend to enjoy it, you'll get all the goodies you want" is the implicit message every time these couples have sex.

You know your relationship is in trouble when faking becomes routine. Faking consistently is like having an illicit bank account where you launder money. Each time you make a deposit (an orgasm), you build up the balance from which you can withdraw later. Several things can be gained by this dubious pact.

To encourage you to think harder about some of your own beliefs as a couple, here are some thoughts that we associate with this pattern. Try them on for size. If any fit, you may have more of an issue in this area than you think.

- Both of us get to think that we are better lovers and more compatible than we really are. Our relationship is marginal, but I can prolong it this way.

- I might get a marriage, money, a lavish lifestyle, children, or trips out of the bargain if I don't mind bragging, sometimes in public, that he's great in bed, even though I would rather sleep, shop, watch television, go to the gym, take a long walk, or do anything other than have sex with him.

- Faking gets sex over quickly. I prefer the "get it up, get it on, and get off" method of having sex. Actually, the faster the sex the better because I'm not concerned with having an orgasm or being satisfied, just avoiding problems.

- I can hide or deny a serious medical or psychiatric problem that I suspect he needs to know about. He doesn't want to face it, either, and that's okay with me.

49

Once you settle into a companionship type of sex life—the kind with infrequent and predictable sex that becomes increasingly unsatisfying and increases your chances of becoming sexually attracted outside of that relationship—the bargain itself begins to feel binding enough to sustain. There's nothing like having an established home, children, grandchildren, and a reputation in the community to keep a couple like this together. Passion and sexual adventure, perhaps once part of each date, are history. But you may not care.

Larry and Susan: Getting Caught in the Act

Larry and Susan are an example of a couple with everything going for them except honesty. They seemed to be perfectly matched sexually. They each had a spontaneous sense of passion and sexual athleticism to spare. They had no inhibitions. If both of them had known how to build a relationship that worked, they might have had it all. Ironically, Larry was the one pretending.

While it is unusual, men can fake it, too. Larry had a secret that he felt he could not tell his new girlfriend, Susan: he masturbated almost daily. With the help of a urologist and sex therapist, he was usually able to control his sex drive. But when Susan suggested they take a vacation to get to know each other better, he was so wildly overjoyed, he made all the arrangements for a two-week vacation in beautiful, isolated Tahiti and stopped his medication.

For what Larry had in mind, he could hardly wait. He and Susan had made love before but not frequently enough for him. On the flight to Tahiti, he could hardly take his eyes off of her. She had chosen to wear a tight-fitting skirt that hugged the curves of her hips like a fast car on a winding mountain road.

That night watching Susan undress was unbelievable to Larry. Once in bed she felt his erection rising immediately.

"My, my, what have we here?"

"Something that will please you all night," Larry replied. He was prepared for one of his best performances.

As their bodies met, Larry rose slightly on his knees and hands and began a gentle, rhythmic motion. After several minutes, Susan's body quivered in a tiny seizure of delight, just as Larry expected. Then when he knew she was ready, he faked his first orgasm. Every time Susan was orgasmic, Larry faked an orgasm, too.

Larry finally allowed himself a real orgasm. The exhausted couple grabbed each other and hung together like their lives depended on it.

Day and night, Larry and Susan made love like the sexual athletes they were. Faking orgasms was Larry's specialty because he had an extraordinary appetite for sex. Unfortunately, the more sex he had, the more he wanted.

After a few days, when Susan was too chafed for penetration, Larry was still ready for more. Susan laughed it off and decided to go shopping. She liked Larry. His style and energy suited her fine, and she was looking forward to sharing some quiet time with him before they returned to the States. But when she came back to the room, there was Larry on the floor masturbating with an inflated sex toy he had brought just in case he needed more sex than he could get otherwise. He thought he was alone.

Susan decided it was time for her to go home, alone.

Negotiating Options ahead of Time

If Susan had known that Larry was trying to manage his medical problem, she might not have been surprised or repulsed by her discovery. As it was, Larry missed a rare opportunity to develop a mutually satisfying sexual relationship.

He could have told Susan he was taking medications to regulate his sex drive. He should have asked her about how much sex she expected on the trip and explained he was looking forward to a lot. With their expectations out in the open, they could have compromised and had sex at a frequency that they both could have enjoyed. Unfortunately, both Larry and Susan missed their chance.

Remember, both partners have a responsibility to take care of their own sexual needs. In this situation, Susan could have taken the initiative at the beginning of their trip to find out what Larry expected and to tell him what she wanted. Talking about sex might have opened the door and given Larry a safe opportunity to come clean about his problem.

Sexual negotiations make both partners feel more comfortable. By negotiating expectations, you show control over your sexuality and at the same time provide greater assurance that your partner's needs will be met.

Facing the Truth about Faking

If both partners understand and accept what's going on, faking pleasure does not have to be a problem. But there is a strong chance that you will improve your relationship if you can avoid having to fake pleasure or orgasms at all.

Open and honest discussions about faking can breathe new life into most relationships, new or old. Remember our prescription for facing anger through conversation. Here's a variation for having a similar dialogue that breaks the silence surrounding faking.

1. **Hold this conversation in a private setting where there's no possibility for interruptions.** Don't let

R_X for Symptoms of an Overactive Sex Drive

If your partner has an overactive sex drive, he may not realize that having more sex will just increase it. You need to know that the more sex he has, the more he will want. Suggest these nonsexual ways to help him satisfy his sex drive without wearing you out:

- Go to the gym together for physical exercise.
- Find a high-nutrition, fitness-oriented diet you like and go on it together.
- Take a meditation class together.
- Learn relaxation techniques. Teach them to him.
- Cuddle with him a lot, without intercourse.
- Learn to give him a massage. Teach him the same techniques to use on you.
- Cook romantic dinners together.

phones, television, drugs, alcohol, or children distract you. For this period of time agreed on by both of you, concentrate on each other in an open, give-and-take manner.

2. **Begin on a positive note.** Start your conversation by talking about what you like about sex with your partner. Don't rush this part of the conversation. Your partner may be searching for reassurance. Feel free to give it, but only where it is due. Is there any mutual interest or desire you share? Is there enough time for arousal, orgasm, or continued intimacy after orgasm for both of you? For example, most people really appreciate a partner who does not fall asleep during or immediately after sex. Express your appreciation by saying it's nice to fall asleep together, if it is.

3. **Ask for the change you want.** After you get a smile or look that gives you feedback on your positive comments, say what needs to be *improved*. Avoid saying what is *wrong*. How you provide constructive criticism will increase the chance that your partner can accept what you are saying. It may be one or more of the positives listed in step 2. Let your partner know.

4. **Give your partner a turn.** Let him say what he likes about making love to you. Then listen to his suggestions about what needs to change.

5. **Reevaluate your sex life on a regular basis.** Remember, the preferred time to do this is not just before or immediately after you have sex. This is an evaluation that needs to take place with all of your clothes on. This is an honest discussion, so you may want to take notes in a special notebook just for this purpose and bring it to every meeting. It's nice to cross off issues when they are no longer a problem. That is progress!

6. **Reassure your partner again.** Be sure your partner knows you want to continue the relationship, even as you are trying to make it better. However, if you can't accomplish this type of communication, even with counseling or sex therapy, and find that you can't agree to work on anything about your sex life, consider the pros and cons of letting go.

When to Hold, When to Fold

When you've met someone with whom you'd like to have a lasting relationship, it is best to be honest about sexual performance. Both of you need to develop a relationship based on how the relationship is *really* working for you. Couples that have been together for a while may require a major overhaul if they have established a pattern of faking pleasure with each other. In counseling, these couples often decide to do the work to stay together precisely because they are established and comfortable with each other. With a genuine commitment to maintaining what they have going for them besides sex, they can usually learn to communicate regularly about sex, too. Once they start to make changes in their sex life, they often discover that the more exciting they are to each other, the less likely either one will be to let go.

Couples that are already emotionally disconnected from each other and can no longer talk to each other honestly about anything, much less sex, may find it's not possible or worthwhile to reconnect.

Finally, it's self-destructive and foolish to expect any good to come from a relationship of faking sexual pleasure if it involves risky sexual acts. Agreeing to being tied up, handcuffed, blindfolded, or to have unprotected sex without using birth control or a condom just to please your partner is playing with fire. Stop before you get burned.

Remember, the best sexual relationships are created with someone who loves you as you are. And the most exasperating are the ones in which you leave your partner in the dark about how you really feel about his sexual performance.

4

Clueless about High-Tech Sex

Secret #4: Sometimes machines can be more risky than people.

Millions of people use vibrators, phone sex services, cybersex, and videos to expand their sexuality. High-tech devices let them fish for true love without putting themselves on the line. That's why we believe that everyone needs at least some understanding about the advantages and the limitations of high-tech sex these days. How's your high tech-sex IQ? This chapter focuses on the advantages and the limitations of these popular technologies.

If high-tech sex sounds extreme to you, think about it for a minute. Nontechnological methods of sexual self-stimulation have existed for thousands of years and can be found in all cultures. Self-stimulation, otherwise known as masturbation, is entirely natural in the animal world. It usually begins in humans at about the age of three; even when their parents disapprove, many children secretly continue to masturbate in private when they are tired or need to be comforted.

Males are more likely than females to stimulate themselves throughout life, especially to quicken their erections. Men tend to masturbate to orgasm more often than women, especially during adolescence or whenever they do not have a sexual partner.

By contrast, girls tend to stop masturbating because of religious and cultural prohibitions, but as a woman's level of education and income rises, her childhood beliefs become less compelling. Like men, educated, upwardly mobile women also like to be what the characters on the long-running television show *Seinfeld* called "masters of their own domain."

And consider this fact: sex videos that include men and women touching themselves and masturbating each other with their hands or mouths are among the most popular in adult sex shops. This leads us to believe that a lot of people who do not stimulate themselves sexually still like to watch other people do it.

But there's a downside to everything under the sun, including self-pleasure. In our experience, individuals who masturbate regularly are often given false information and learn inferior techniques by trial and error. They usually shy away from talking about what they're doing because they fear being caught and labeled as a "freak" by their family and friends. And some people, including all children, are too emotionally vulnerable to handle the consequences of too much stimulation too early in their sexual development.

Also, if you don't know what you're doing, an independent approach to turning yourself on can make it harder to enjoy sex with a partner. That's what almost happened to our patient, Cynthia. Her story represents both the many pluses and a few necessary cautions associated with a high-tech approach to sexual pleasure.

Cynthia and "Walter": Why Women Love Vibrators

Cynthia, a thirty-something African American born in Covington, Georgia, joined a midsized company in Chicago. She loved her job, except for one big drawback. At her level of corporate management, she had little opportunity to meet men who were interested in her as a woman. She hired or fired most of the people she worked with. While she enjoyed the power of her position, it was definitely taking a toll on her love life.

After several failed attempts at romance, Cynthia accepted the fact that she might be single forever, but she had decided she wasn't going to let the absence of a partner deprive her of the kind of pleasure she saw pictured in women's magazines and read about in romance novels. She thought of herself as a take-charge type of woman. But what was a single woman supposed to do about sex when she refused to sleep with just anyone to get what she needed?

Like many women, she had been raised to expect that a man would come riding by, scoop her up, and take her away to a storybook life. She was expecting a beautiful house, car, children, and mad passionate sex when the kids went to bed. That dream had not come true yet so Cynthia used her managerial skills to solve her sexual problem. She planned to become orgasmic all by herself.

One day, Cynthia took a taxi to a pleasure store in the city to buy herself the most elaborate, quiet, and natural-looking vibrator she could find. Vibrators are motorized dildos. They can help you relax and give you sexual pleasure and sometimes orgasms, whether you have a partner or not. You can purchase vibrators in all shapes, sizes, and colors at adult sex shops or stores that specialize in relaxation devices.

It was a tough trip down to the sex shop, because this was not how Cynthia had been raised. She grew up spending most of her Sundays and Wednesdays in church. While some religions prohibit masturbation, Cynthia's did not condemn it or say much about it at all. But religious and cultural beliefs are the primary reason guilt and shame is associated with self-stimulation.

She began one night with a soothing bubble bath, accompanied by incense, candles, and soft music. Then she placed a warm, fluffy towel on her bed and sat down. After stroking her body to the point of arousal, Cynthia brought out "Walter," her vibrator.

This was when she got off track. She fumbled with the device, lost her concentration on her sexy mood, and startled herself as Walter hummed away. She could not figure out how to maintain her level of arousal and use the vibrator at the same time. After two frustrating weeks of getting to the same level of arousal and not "coming," she decided to consult us.

We suggested that Cynthia use her hand less and her vibrator more every day for a week. We also asked her to record her progress in her diary. Each day, she detailed how much stimulation she needed for arousal and the length of time it took to evoke those feelings.

With this information, we helped her customize a method of reaching an orgasm whenever she wanted, whether she was tired, relaxed, in a hurry, or really tense. This was mainly a matter of showing her the difference between the onset of sexual pleasure and the beginning of sexual arousal, and how to recalibrate the way she timed and paced those events. With daily practice, she became more and more adept at getting the results she wanted.

Cynthia loved to fantasize that Denzel Washington was touching her. She rented his romantic movies and practiced with Walter at the same time she watched. She also learned a lot about her body. It was a real breakthrough when she discovered that she liked direct stimulation to her clitoris.

In about three weeks, her daily practice paid off. At first

she wasn't really sure what was happening, but she had a warm feeling every time she used Walter for about thirty minutes, while touching her breasts. This warm sensation would gradually build in her genital area, giving her the effect of a slow release of tension and a calming, pleasurable sensation.

With our help, she was able to identify that indeed she had become orgasmic. She was delighted and sometimes would go home at noon, put Walter to work, have an orgasm, and go back to work calmer and ready for a busy afternoon. Cynthia was soon able to climax in less than fifteen minutes. She also discovered that she liked having fast sex—a mechanical quickie. She didn't need to talk to anyone, be nice, waste precious time, or worry about satisfying anyone but herself. She didn't have to remind anyone to "Call me!" She didn't have to hunt Walter down—he lived in her lingerie drawer.

Cynthia and Paul: Changing a High-Tech Script

Just when Cynthia thought she had her sexual needs under control, she met a man who stole her heart, a new "rookie" in town. Paul had recently been transferred from the corporate office in Columbus, Ohio, and knew very few people in Chicago. He and Cynthia were introduced and hit it off right away. They had a lot in common and talked business over lunch almost daily. Soon they realized there was more to their lunches than business, and they began to date.

By this time, Paul knew that what he wanted was a relationship that could possibly lead to something lasting. Cynthia was noncommittal at first, but his sincerity and warmth were convincing, and after a while, Cynthia agreed to sex.

Some of our patients balk at getting tested for sexually transmitted diseases (STDs) and HIV. Cynthia and Paul were too smart for that. They got the tests, and after examining each

R$_X$ for Learning to Use a Vibrator

Week One

- Using your hand, locate the areas of your genitals that are pleasing to touch. Slowly and gently explore the shape of your outer and inner labia. Move your hand up to your clitoris and leave it there, keeping the pressure light but constant on your body until the clitoris begins to grow hard.

- Practice touching these areas with your hand for pleasure only, once a day.

Week Two

- Now, using your vibrator, repeat the process of Week One. Determine the level of vibration you enjoy: slow, fast, light, or heavy.

- Practice touching yourself with your vibrator for pleasure only, no more than once a day.

Week Three

- Using your vibrator, find the level of touch that makes you sexually aroused. You will know because your nipples will become erect or your breathing will grow deeper. Always relax, breathing deeply.

- Note how long it takes to feel first pleasure and then arousal. Practice no more than once a day.

- Practice enhancing your pleasure after arousal. Tense all your muscles and then relax them again. With practice, you can repeat this "body squeeze" exercise several times with even better results.

Warning: You can become infected with sexually transmitted diseases if you share the dildo or vibrator with others. Cleaning it with alcohol, bleach, or a dildo cleanser after each use will minimize this problem. Stop use until healing occurs to avoid painful sex if you become chafed or bruised, or get rashes.

other's written results, determined to share the responsibility of protecting each other and their relationship from unintended consequences of sex. They selected a diaphragm for her and condoms for him.

Now they were ready for sex. They had eliminated unnecessary risk and anxiety and given their sexual relationship the best chance to succeed. But in another way, the challenge had just begun. Their first night together, Paul took his time kissing and touching Cynthia, but after forty-five minutes of cuddling, she was about to scream. For Cynthia, this unusually thoughtful man was taking way too long to get to intercourse.

What happened? Cynthia was out of practice with a human partner. Paul slowed down, looking at her expression.

"What's the matter?"

Cynthia had to decide right then whether to tell Paul the truth or pretend that she was enjoying the experience, which she clearly was not. Cynthia decided to keep her secret. She told Paul she would need more time before they had intercourse.

They tried again the next evening. Once again, Cynthia found herself frustrated without Walter's usual, expert touch to bring on an orgasm. Adding to that problem, she also realized she feared the potential pain and discomfort adjusting to the size of Paul's penis. She really just wanted to get the whole thing over with.

She and Paul had a pretty big argument on Saturday night (one that Cynthia started) and Paul left early Sunday morning. He was clueless about what was happening, and Cynthia was clueless about how and even *if* she could be honest with him.

It didn't take long for Cynthia to realize that she did not want to let Paul get away. She took a chance and told him the truth about her sexual script of fast sex and how it was interfering with their sex life. To her amazed relief, he listened and understood.

Together, they planned a strategy to wean her off Walter. Trust in each other helped them withstand their sexual differences and work them out.

"Call it what it is, Cyn," Paul insisted. "I'm real, that vibrator is only a substitute."

He was right. With time, Paul took Walter's place. Almost.

Every now and then, Cynthia spent an afternoon with Walter, just for old time's sake. As long as she kept batteries in store, she would always have Walter for those occasions when Paul was not interested or available.

The Inside Story: Human vs. Mechanical Sex Partners

Everyone has a pace at which they naturally like to make love. Part of the challenge for human couples is discovering and getting in sync with each other's preferred pace and timing. Cynthia's natural pace had been thrown off by the daily use of a vibrator. She had become accustomed to a lifestyle of mechanical, or recipe, sex. With Walter she had learned what to do to get the outcome she wanted. She did not know how to adapt to the more creative but slower style of having sex with a human partner.

Fortunately, Cynthia sought professional advice to solve this problem. We wish more people had Cynthia's can-do attitude. If you isolate yourself from advisors and confidants, it's extremely easy to remain clueless when the solution is right at hand. If you become orgasmic very easily with vibrators, you may find that you, too, need help in learning how to enjoy human sexual contact again, or for the first time.

First of all, being in a relationship does not mean that you have to give up the use of a vibrator. Cynthia's problem was not that she had two methods of sexual gratification, but that she had not modified her pattern. Now she needed a different script.

R$_X$ for Changing Your Script

To enjoy sex in a human relationship after perfecting the vibrator habit, you'll need to practice patience while learning to adopt a different sexual pace and lifestyle. Here's how to begin the process:

- **Start looking for other ways besides sex to release tension,** such as relaxation, meditation, or exercise.

- **Use your vibrator less and less each week.**

- **Increase touching the breasts and genitals with your hands** until you can reach sexual pleasure and arousal manually.

- **Start spending some time touching yourself or being touched by a partner and not having an orgasm.** The point is to become more aware of the fact that every sexual encounter does not necessarily have to end in a climax to end in pleasure.

- **Do Kegel exercises** by alternately relaxing and contracting the vaginal muscles. They are great practice to prepare for vaginal penetration. The result may be more intense orgasms. Kegel exercises are especially beneficial for women who have never had sex or those who are postmenopausal and are losing their vaginal elasticity because of age and the lack of estrogen. See page 28 for instructions on Kegel exercises.

Remember This Clue

The vagina is surrounded by muscle that needs to be exercised and toned. If it is going to perform well, you have to keep it in good shape.

Being accustomed to one form of stimulation exclusively makes it more challenging to adapt to both, but not impossible.

Here's what she needed to know:

- Vibrators can maintain a steady rhythm. Humans tend to alter their rhythm and become tired after a while.

- Vibrators can be turned off when you get excited. A human partner may want to continue arousing you or be aroused by you. Humans are much more demanding than machines.

- Finally, your human partner may not be interested in sex when you are.

Luis's Story: Phone Sex, Why It Works, and Why It Goes Wrong

Like Cynthia, Luis was looking for a solution to a sexual problem that was out of control. And just like Cynthia, he chose a popular high-tech method that, on the surface, seemed to perfectly fit his needs. Luis was one of the millions of people without exciting sexual partners who are increasingly drawn to phone sex.

This medium allows you to use your fantasy to create an environment in which you and a consenting partner have sex (usually masturbation) that both of you engage in (by yourselves) and describe to each other during a phone call.

There are several positive features of phone sex for people who can accept that this is a fantasy-driven method of sexual gratification. For instance, you can avoid the risks of unintended pregnancies and STD and HIV infection since there is usually no physical contact. You don't have to go out on social dates. And you can either pretend you have a relationship or not, as you wish, as long as you remember it's all a pay-to-play game between consenting partners.

But phone sex can easily create unrealistic expectations. For example, it's not hard to get carried away when a phone partner says:

"Nice to hear from you again. I enjoyed our last conversation, more than any of the others."

But it doesn't mean you're popular.

Or "You are so sexy. I just came and came when I talked with you."

It doesn't mean you have good or even adequate sexual skills.

Or "I was afraid that you would call someone else. I have gotten used to your calls. Please call me tomorrow."

These scripts are just another payday for your partner, especially if all he or she knows about you is based on telephone or Internet conversations.

For an isolated person who may not have very good social skills, who has few friends and no sexual contact, those phone partners sound very convincing, though. That was Luis's high-tech problem.

This sixteen-year-old, first-generation Filipino American was on the dean's list but not for getting good grades. He was one class away from failing out of school and in big trouble at home. He had stolen his father's credit card to charge two-hour phone sex conversations each night. Most adolescents call phone sex numbers because they want to see how powerful a "lover" they can be without having to suffer rejection by an actual person. Others use phone sex for more adult reasons, namely, they simply want sex and lack willing partners. The phone enables them to fantasize about sexual practices that they can't or won't be involved with a regular partner. Luis tearfully explained to us:

My parents are very religious and very strict. They don't know that I am gay, so I have to find ways to take care of my needs.

Every night my phone partner Raul and I talk end-lessly about my problems. He makes me feel good and then we talk sexy to each other. I masturbate while he is talking to me and pretend that he is touching me. When it's over, I feel better for a while. Then I am ashamed because I know what my parents would think and I know that they are just working-class people. They can't pay this bill.

At a family meeting, we helped Luis "come out" to his parents. They declared a truce about his homosexuality; but his habit of indirect sexual contact escalated.

Increasingly, Luis enjoyed overhearing or seeing people having sex. Rather than having actual physical contact with a partner, Luis frequented adult bookstores where he could see "peep shows" with men having sex with other men, while he masturbated. Rather than risk getting arrested for indecent behavior in public places, Luis and his partner began to role-play the scenes that Luis found exciting. They would have phone sex and then meet. If they had kept it to an occasional encounter, it would have been a safe, exciting way to manage a sexual pattern that was satisfying for them both, but it got out of control.

Luis was overwhelmed trying to come to grips with his sexuality and fears of being rejected because he was gay. While he chose to hide his sex life, he was using a very public means of sexual gratification—a phone sex line. He was not aware that a phone sex partner could record their conversations and use those tapes to obtain money or other sexual favors from him. To reduce his use of phone sex or indirect sexual gratification, he would have to learn how to depend on it less. This method of desensitization to one form of gratification was similar to what Cynthia accomplished when she became less dependent on her vibrator.

Men often fantasize about good sex or being good sexual partners. The fantasy of having a penis two feet long, hard as steel, and ever ready can easily be reinforced during phone sex. This is a lure for men because our society has such well-defined roles for masculinity. Overcoming sexual insecurity by affirming their male identities and pursuing sexual gratification can easily be the most destructive parts of men's lives.

Phone sex is exciting because you can only hear your partner. The rest of the script you create for yourself. The more you fantasize about your sexual partner, what they are like, and how much they are turned on by you, the more you enter your ideal world of sexual gratification. You focus on what you would like to be real rather than what actually is.

Straight men are just as prone to sexual fantasies about their performance because they so seldom talk with anyone about their bodies, their sexuality, or how they are performing. If these men have phone sex routinely, they may be the last ones to know that their actual performance leaves a lot to be desired.

Get a Clue

Remember, you can have sex without trust, respect, closeness, intimacy, and open communication, but not a healthy sexual relationship. It is really difficult, if not impossible, to get honest feedback about your sexual performance with a phone sex partner, unless they have had actual contact with you.

Ray, Cindi, and Shaun: High-Tech Cheating

While you may not always pay money to have sex over the phone, it can be costly in other ways. Ray was a good example. A married, athletic auto mechanic from Atlanta, he was hardly a teenager, but he loved a daily phone date during his lunch hour with Cindi, a woman he had met in a bar. Unlike his wife, Shaun, Cindi was adventuresome.

"Talking to Cindi every day makes me feel like a man. I can say things to her that I can't say to Shaun." Ray had two women as sexual partners and preferred the one who was not his wife. He was defining his manhood by his ability to sound and feel sexy, and he needed daily reinforcement.

Ray thought these daily sexual treats did not qualify as adultery because he was only having virtual sex with Cindi. However, his sexual energy was drained and he was less interested in sex with Shaun. She became worried that he was having an affair. Ray and Shaun came to therapy to settle their disagreement about Ray's activities: was phone sex adultery?

Ray was surprised to find that Shaun considered his behavior adulterous and was confused about why he was no longer interested in her sexually. She was deeply hurt that he went outside the relationship for his sexual gratification, but she did not want a divorce. She wanted to fight for him.

It became clear that communication and not sex was at the heart of their problems. When Shaun heard what Ray wanted, she agreed to be more open and to try new things that they both felt would be exciting and new to their relationship. Ray accepted that it was his responsibility to end his relationship with Cindi and tell Shaun what he liked so that they had a chance to develop a new sexual pattern together.

Unfortunately, it took the near collapse of their marriage for Ray and Shaun to start communicating about their sex life. But fortunately, it wasn't too late.

> ## R$_x$: Try This Problem-Solving Exercise
>
> Try this technique when you and your partner need to do some problem-solving together.
> - **In round one,** agree that you will talk for fifteen minutes while your partner listens. Then switch places. Let your partner talk for fifteen minutes while you listen.
>
> - **In round two,** each partner gets ten minutes to repeat what they heard the other say. Allow each other five minutes to clarify what you intended to communicate.

Cybersex Appeal

Cybersex is sexual interaction between two or more people in order to become aroused and satisfied sexually through immediate messages on the Internet. Meeting people and establishing relationships over the Internet presents many opportunities and challenges. You can:

- Attract potential friends, dates, or partners from a worldwide pool. Alone, few if any individuals could accomplish this feat.

- Pass messages back and forth in such a quick and powerful way that you feel that electricity is binding the two of you together.

- Create a personality, common interests, friendship, and a sense of trust on the Internet and never come face-to-face with the person you have these feelings for.

- Create an environment that can look and seem so real that you can evoke the same feelings that you may experience if you were having sex. You can create physical bodies and an entire physical space in which two people have sex.

Newsgroups or chat rooms give people the sense that they belong to a group and are having a conversation on a topic that they all want to discuss. Sometimes the name of the group or room provides you with enough information to infer what the topic of discussion will be. An article to read or a topic can be posted for those who care to respond and provide comments. Personal ads can be so much more effective when you can "write" to your potential date or cyber pal. Users in a chat room can split off and have a private conversation.

Similar to telephone sex, cybersex users can find sexual pleasure regardless of how they look or what they are really like. The cyberspace image does not have to be real. However, using the Internet to talk about sex, meet potential partners, or develop chat buddies is far more powerful than phone sex because you can create a virtual environment that seems real enough to justify the two of you being together.

Because of these reasons, the potential for abuse is high. Virtual friendships can be confusing, especially to children, adolescents, and vulnerable people who are lonely, shy, and looking for attention, or those who think they are unattractive or have physical disabilities. Corrine was such a person.

Corrine's Story: In over Her Head

Corrine was a white, smart fifteen-year-old, with a face not likely to be seen in *Seventeen* magazine. Frozen out of the in-crowd at school, she started playing computer sex games for comfort and companionship. She joined a chat room hoping to find cyber pals and struck up an acquaintance with Julian.

After several days of playing games, Julian asked for her phone number. They started having phone sex regularly. When Julian asked to meet her, she refused. She was afraid he would find her as unattractive as everyone else did and break off their relationship. When he threatened to do just that, Corrine agreed to meet at a movie. She hoped that the dark theater would hide her appearance.

She was nervous and got there early. They were supposed to sit on the left side in the back but she sat in the middle section and kept looking to see Julian when he arrived. She had noticed a stranger on the opposite side where they were to meet. Halfway through the movie Corrine went to their meeting place and the stranger moved into the seat next to her. He said he was Julian and wanted to see her before he showed himself. They were playing games again, and Corrine was amused. He was older than he had described himself to be. In fact, neither of them looked anything like they described, but neither seemed to care. He put his arm around her and gave her a kiss on the cheek, and thanked her for coming. Julian told her she was beautiful, something she didn't expect but desperately wanted to hear. They shared popcorn and watched the rest of the movie when suddenly Julian asked her to go outside so they could talk.

Flattered by his compliments and attention, Corrine dismissed other concerns about going places with strangers and agreed. They talked outside and that evening had phone sex. This time Corrine had a face to put with Julian's voice, which heightened her excitement. They met again the next Saturday and Corrine let Julian kiss and touch her. Now she felt she was as good or better than the girls at school. She had a boyfriend.

On their next date, Julian took Corrine to a party. But he was more forceful this time: he kissed Corrine and felt under her dress. She asked him to stop, but he wouldn't. He was into her panties and she started to cry. Nobody, particularly Julian, seemed to notice her distress. She begged him to let her go to the bathroom to put in a diaphragm, something she heard the other girls at school say. Julian told her to hurry up. Corrine got through the door, into the street, and ran all the way home. Her parents would have never understood what she was willing to do to be liked, so she never told them.

The Inside Story

With millions of young and vulnerable users, the Internet provides people with unusual appetites an opportunity to meet people who might be potential victims. It attracts predators who may be seeking sexual contact rather than a relationship and gives them a chance to meet more prey.

Among the most common abusers are paraphiles, people who have recurrent, intense, sexually arousing fantasies, sexual urges, or behaviors that involve nonhuman objects such as animals. They often advertise over the Internet for work on farms in order to have access to chickens, horses, cows, and sheep. We mention them here because paraphiles also have sexual urges for children and other nonconsenting people.

Pedophiles are another common type of Internet predator. They are sexually aroused through sexual activity with children and often seek out opportunities to be around children in the workplace, schools, churches, or in families. They often use chat rooms and newsgroups to seek out individuals who can help them to gain access to their sources of sexual gratification.

Research shows that in chat rooms or newsgroups, fewer than one in ten participants are really youths. Of people who are online, one in four is a pornographer attempting to sell material or to find new recruits for videos, movies, or magazines.

The Internet is the venue through which people can easily exploit or be exploited for sex. No matter the potential hazards, however, it will grow in popularity as long as it provides access to sexual materials and partners.

Sue-Lin: Turned on and Turned off by Videos

Videos offer the advantage of supplanting human interactions and going straight for titillation. Once it was books that excited people's sexual imaginations. Today, it's videos. Soft-porn videos feature mild to moderately risky sexual acts between people. Hard-porn videos graphically portray highly risky sexual acts between people or animals. Best-sellers worldwide offer private access to visual and auditory sexual stimulation that no book can offer.

The advantage of videos is that you can use your fantasy and imagine yourself in dangerous sex scenes without risking your life. Or you can identify with characters portrayed as innocent, everyday people "turned on" or "turned off." If you have established personal boundaries for safety that cannot be compromised by your need to find love and be loved, watching videos may do no harm to you if they do no harm to others.

But, in fact, the actors could be your neighbors. The only difference is that the actors have erased the ethical, physical, and emotional boundaries between life and pornography that you enjoy. The process by which this happens to them is degrading and regrettable, if understandable.

Sue-Lin, one of our patients, told us the story of how she crossed the line. When we met her, she was a twenty-six-year-old Chinese immigrant housewife. Years before, when Sue-Lin was fifteen, her parents answered an ad in a paper from an established American businessman seeking a wife to live with him in the United States. When Sue-Lin agreed to marry him, he deposited a large sum of money in a bank account for her family—more money than her father had ever made before. She earned respect from her parents but had made a contract with the devil. Her husband would film her performing all kinds of acts with him, including oral (she put his penis in her mouth) and anal sex (he put his penis in her anus). He would also

perform "golden or brown showers" (he would urinate or defe-
cate on her). After filming these acts, he would watch them and
masturbate.

Sue-Lin begged him not to tape their sex acts, for fear that
he might show them to her parents or try to blackmail her. He
had already threatened to do just that if she left him. She felt
trapped in the marriage and unable to protect herself from her
husband's sexual advances until she began to pay attention to
the porno videos that her husband rented. She realized that she
was doing all of the things that the actors in the videos were
doing—except they were getting paid. She decided that her
ticket to freedom was to become a porno star.

Sue-Lin became a part of the adult movie industry and
continues to be one of the highest paid stars in the business. She
says she has no regrets.

Think about your own lifestyle and choices. Remember,
you do have a choice. You control the role technology plays in
your sex life. But whatever you decide, remember these do's and
don'ts:

1. **Don't forget who you are.** Getting to know someone per-
    sonally and for a long period of time is still the only way
    to establish genuine bonds. To have a safe, healthy rela-
    tionship, partners must know each other's real identities.
    Modern technology can speed up the process of commu-
    nication but not replace it. The best relationships still begin
    with friendships and do not require you to rush or feel
    pressured or forced to please your partner.

2. **Don't forget your people skills.** Learn how to listen and
    to stimulate conversation that interests you and others.
    Practice connecting with others in a sincere and honest
    way, on the phone and in daily life. Practice these skills
    each day and you're bound to improve your ability to be
    personal, warm, and real in sex, too.

3. **Do be clear about what you are trying to avoid or gain.** If you are trying to avoid spending time on relationships or facing rejection by your partner, sexual devices are not the answer. You have to deal with your fears first. If you don't, high-tech sex can do more harm than good.

4. **Don't be deluded by a false sense of security.** If you have difficulty making friends and developing relationships, the Internet may leave you believing that you have overcome these problems when people respond to your e-mails.

5. **Do verify an interested person's history.** Do a background check before you attempt to establish a relationship with someone you met online. A responsible person will understand and not be put off by your need for more information.

6. **Do pay attention to the depth of your feelings.** Your feelings are an important indicator that this is a relationship that deserves more time to see if it can develop into something more lasting. If your attraction is based on sexual urges, voice tone, or the ability to be sexy or say warm and loving things, you need much more information in order to decide whether you are in a relationship based only on mutual physical attraction. It is most important to understand the basis of your sexual attraction.

7. **Do make sure you are acting out your own script instead of your partner's.** This is especially important when nothing requires you to be in the same physical space as the person to whom you are attracted. Share your feelings with someone who knows you—preferably someone older and wiser, who cares about you. They also need to meet the person that you like and give you their opinion about how real the relationship is. Ask them to honestly tell

you if you are in denial and want a relationship so badly that you can't really use good judgment. It is also possible that in spite of all that you try to do, you won't know everything that you should to protect yourself. You can only know a person as well as they know themselves. When you see behaviors that contradict what you expected, take that information seriously. Actions really do speak louder than words.

8. **Don't invest too much of yourself in the relationship.** Ask yourself, "Is this what I want in five years?" If it is not, you may just be transitioning from this relationship to a more meaningful relationship that will come later in life. Be careful not to disclose too much personal information or make promises that you can't or won't keep in five years. Part of the challenge of understanding yourself is learning when to change and when to let go, including being in a virtual world.

5

Clueless about Your Body's Potential

Secret #5: Don't give up trying when your body won't do what you want. Sexual pleasure is always possible.

What happens when you can't have sex the way you want to anymore? Or when it seems as if you can no longer have sex at all? Many people suffer in silence because they don't know what to do. Some don't want to face the facts. Others are too embarrassed to try to work with their sexual partners toward a solution.

We believe that nothing should prevent you from expressing the love you feel and getting sexual love in return. If sexual dysfunction, hypertension, diabetes, fibroids, injury, or any other physical problem threatens your sex life, you can still make love. If any of the key elements of sexual response are missing from your experience with someone you love, you can still improve your sex life together. This chapter will help you identify and make the necessary changes before your relationship is seriously affected.

Earlier, we touched on the nature of human sexual response. We need to expand on this now. To help jog your memory, the elements are:

- **Desire:** Do you feel you have an adequate level of interest, willingness, and need for sex?
- **Excitement:** Does your partner achieve an erect penis with reasonable ease for his age? Do you get an erect clitoris, hard breast nipples, or vaginal lubrication as signals of sexual excitement or arousal?
- **Orgasm:** With the proper stimulation, do you experience the crescendo and peak of sexual activity or ejaculation?
- **Resolution:** When your body returns to its normal state after sex, do you experience regular breathing and a noticeably lower heart rate?
- **Sexual satisfaction:** Do you have a sense that the result of the entire sexual experience is pleasant?

The repeated lack of one or more of these elements over time can result in:

- Low sexual desire or no interest in sex (hypoactive sexual desire disorder)
- Inability to experience orgasm, climax, or ejaculate (orgasmic disorder)
- Inability to achieve an erection hard enough to penetrate (erectile disorder)

While individual sexual responses differ according to age, cultural background, religious beliefs about sex, drugs, alcohol, health problems, and past sexual experiences and their physical and psychological effects, these problems are frequently the reason why people find themselves desperate for a sex life that works.

Chanté and Jean Claude: Clueless about Sexual Desire

Low sexual desire affects about 43 percent of women at some point in their lives. It is most common in women shortly before and after menopause when the body's estrogen levels are low. Symptoms can include a persistent absence of sexual thoughts and fantasies.

Chanté was only twenty-eight years old when she discovered that she had a problem. She had met Jean Claude, a Swiss recording agent, at a church revival. Their mission work took them all over the world to spread the gospel and a message of celibacy before marriage. They deeply loved each other, and became engaged.

But on their wedding night, Jean Claude had to coax Chanté out of the bathroom and into bed. She insisted they pray. For twenty minutes Jean Claude went along with the program.

"Chanté, don't you want to have sex?" Jean Claude finally asked gently.

"Actually . . . no, I'm afraid and I'm really not interested in having sex," Chanté confessed. "I just love being with you, talking to you, and working with you. I could live with you forever without having sex if you would agree to that." She was stunned as the words tumbled out. There, she had admitted it.

Jean Claude looked at her in amazement, but he was so touched by her honesty, he just hugged her. Eventually, they fell asleep.

When Chanté and Jean Claude came to therapy six months later, they had yet to have sexual intercourse. Both of them were depressed and unhappy. After we took a careful history, it became clear that Chanté really did not know how to become sexually excited. She had no interest or desire for sexual intercourse and did not masturbate or stimulate herself in any way. She had learned to ignore any feelings of arousal or excitement. She had no sexual dreams or fantasies.

Because Chanté wanted to change, we began a step-by-step approach in sex therapy that helped her notice and express her hidden sexuality.

Enjoy Your Body's Response

Chanté and Jean Claude were twenty minutes late for therapy after taking the sixth step. They were very quiet when they arrived.

"What's the matter?" we asked, expecting that something terrible might have happened.

"We made a mistake!" Chanté replied. She seemed distressed. "We were doing the homework and got too excited. One thing led to another and we had sex. Jean Claude didn't move a lot, but he was inside me."

"What was the mistake?" we asked with relief.

"We had sex, and you told us not to."

"Actually, we said don't have sex until further notice. You just served notice."

Relieved, they smiled.

"What was it like?" we asked.

"Divine!"

"Well then, amen." We all laughed.

Marta and Jerry: When Pain Affects Desire

Women do not usually go to a doctor because of a decrease in sexual desire but because of related problems, such as painful sex (dyspareunia). Dyspareunia occurs in 11 to 14 percent of all women and can have a direct affect on relationships. If

R$_x$ for Healing Low Desire: Six Homework Assignments

If you have experienced problems in becoming sexually excited, you can actually do a lot to help yourself to sexual arousal with the following program of action steps. If they do not help, it's a sign that you may need sex therapy with a professional to make sex work for both of you.

Here are the six steps to sexual arousal that put Chanté on the path to a lasting and deeply transforming result. These may help you and your partner explore your full potential for interest and desire for sexual pleasure. Allow yourself several weeks to complete the steps. Practice not rushing.

Step One

Learn how to identify pleasant, sensuous, and sexy feelings, and identify situations that make you feel that way. You don't need to go out of your way to create these feelings. Just pay attention to what your brain and body are saying to you naturally during the day and night. You may be surprised to find that you respond a bit more often than you think to pleasant, sexy stimuli.

Step Two

Tell your partner he has to promise to avoid trying to have sexual intercourse with you until further notice. His big reward is coming later. Agree to kiss and hug but not to touch each other's genitals. For now, sexual excitement is your primary goal. You are learning to distinguish between excitement and intercourse.

Step Three

Each night, have conversations with your partner about what you are learning about sexual excitement and how you respond to it. You want your partner to feel a part of your new experience. Share it with him enthusiastically.

Step Four

Search for things that affect your senses pleasurably. Chanté was a visual person. Romantic movies and books and certain magazines made her feel good, sensuous, and sexy. Try different stimuli such as aromas and scents, flowers and candles, running water and hot tubs, pictures, sunbathing, different types of music, even incense.

Many people find that high-protein meals and exercise increase sexual desire. Eventually you'll know a lot more about what does and what doesn't turn you on. Treat yourself to new experiences. Experiment with the feel of soft fabrics against your skin, caressing different parts of your body, wearing sexy lingerie, looking at your body in a mirror, and buying clothes in colors that appeal to you.

Rent videos of general-distribution movies with erotic or romantic themes. Or experiment with quiet lush or exotic restaurants. Try cooking special dinners for two at home. The possibilities are limitless; if you run out of ideas, look for more in magazines.

Step Five

Invite your partner to join you in this process now. Based on what you've learned, teach him how to make you feel good, sensuous, and sexy. Chanté and Jean Claude had weekly dates at home. Chanté had arranged the furniture and lighting in a way that pleased her senses. In her favorite room, they would "make out," including kissing. We had also encouraged them to touch each other's genitals. Chanté loved to have Jean Claude touch her breasts and the lips of her vagina. Remember, no intercourse is recommended yet.

> **Step Six**
>
> In your homework now you can touch each other any-
> where, including the genitals, and do whatever you
> think might stimulate you to get ready for sex.

penetrating the vagina causes pain, low sexual desire often results. Such was the case for Marta.

Marta is an attractive married woman in her late fifties. She grew up in Oklahoma and relocated to California after marriage. Marta was diagnosed with hypoactive sexual desire because of involuntary spasms at the opening of her vagina dur- ing intercourse (vaginismus). Rarely did she have sex without pain. As a result, she had few long-term relationships before marriage and had never initiated sex or masturbated. She was a passive sex partner. Becoming sexually excited was not easy for her.

Her husband, Jerry, became exhausted when he attempted to get her ready for sex. Marta described him as being very patient. But sex had become so painful she would bite her lip and try to get it over with as soon as possible. She taught Jerry to come quickly. But the last time they had sex, the pain became so unbearable that Marta actually passed out.

Frightened and fearing she would lose him, Marta reluc- tantly told Jerry about her problem and suggested he mastur- bate or use prostitutes. Jerry, angry and rejected, told her to see the doctor and began to avoid physical contact with her. He didn't want to hurt her or frustrate himself.

When we saw Marta, we realized that her complaint was just the tip of the iceberg. We know by now that if a doctor's office visit has anything to do with sex, relationship problems are also present. We were right again. Physically, Marta needed help to reduce her fear of painful sex. We taught her to control the involuntary spasms of her vagina. Her partner, Jerry, had some things to learn, too.

Exercise Helps

If you experience painful penetration, have a physical examination to rule out a serious medical problem. Then try this: using a dildo, practice controlling the muscles of your vagina with Kegel exercises (opening and closing the vagina). When your control increases to a point where you feel comfortable, ask your partner to practice entering your vagina. Help him recognize the feeling of your vagina when you relax those muscles. (See chapter 1 for more information about Kegel exercises.)

Healing Your Relationship:
Advice for Both of You

Many sexual partners try to hide low sexual desire, like Marta did. When a woman feels pressured to perform sexually, other problems like painful sex or getting an infection can result. Eventually, she ends up losing a partner as well as her sexual health.

This is one more reason why couples need to be open and honest with each other about sexual problems. Each partner needs to pay constant attention to the other to avoid someone suffering in silence if they are really not enjoying sex.

If your partner's sexual appetite or libido is greater or less than yours, it's okay to take responsibility for your unmet sexual needs through abstinence or masturbation. Communicating about sex and reaching compromises is critical to a healthy relationship. This means each of you needs to feel comfortable in discussing sex.

Men, if it takes extra time to tell your partner what you want or to find out when she's ready for penetration, that's okay. She probably also needs more intimacy from you, including talking, kissing, hugging, and touching. Shower her with warm and tender physical contact. She may relax more, and return the affection.

Remember These Important Clues

When you experience low desire or pain:

- Don't ignore what you suspect might be wrong.

- Don't discount your partner's feelings.

- Don't let your partner put you down (call you a lousy lover or selfish) or demean you in any way.

- Don't let your partner hurt you. If you are in pain but feel tempted to ask him to go ahead and hurt you, don't do it. There is nowhere to go when you lose honesty in your relationship, except to grow further apart.

Gui: Down Low with Premature Ejaculation

Premature ejaculation, or PE, which occurs in one in five men, is quick sex at its worst. Ejaculation not only comes early, it can occur during sexual foreplay or when your partner is attempting penetration. Gui was such a partner.

He was a handsome, eighteen-year-old French exchange student on the "down low," meaning he was getting all the action he could handle, having sex with girls in his class and with boys, too. Nobody except a few of his "fuck buddies" knew that he was bisexual.

Gui had a sexual problem that was really depressing him. He would ejaculate just as he was about to have intercourse with girls. He would laugh it off and explain that he just got "too excited," but it happened all the time. When he was getting "blown" or having oral sex with guys, it seemed less of a problem.

"Am I just gay? Why do I have this problem with girls? How can I find out?" he asked one day.

Our conversation went like this:

"You've got some important questions to answer about your sexual performance, but maybe your sexuality is bothering you more than your performance. You are not telling the girls you have sex with that you also have sex with guys, but do the guys know about the girls?" we asked.

"Yeah. They all do the same thing. We just keep each other's secrets."

"Is that okay for you to hide the truth about who you are from some of your sexual partners but not others?"

"No. I'm not ashamed of being bisexual," he replied.

"Then why hide? Give each of your partners the 411 and then you both decide where you want to take the relationship."

"But some of the girls will think I'm gay and won't have sex with me."

"Yes . . . and?"

"I guess that's okay."

"If you hide, you are less likely to use condoms and protect your partner from any disease that you or they might have. Tell the truth, Gui, and see what happens."

Well, change didn't happen overnight, but slowly Gui began to tell all of his sexual partners about his bisexuality. If they agreed to have sex, he was able to relax, take his time, and delay ejaculation. He taught some partners the squeeze technique, which also helped him to last longer (see chapter 2).

Germaine: The Problem with Self-Medicating for PE

Other problems with PE are more difficult to resolve. Such was the case with Germaine, a twenty-year-old Italian medical student. He had always hidden his failure to perform sexually. He was anxious to learn as much as he could about the male sexual response because his sex life was going nowhere. His last girlfriend actually thought it was funny when he took over half an hour rubbing against her to get an erection and then ejaculated while trying to enter her vagina. No more humiliation for him. He was going to put his smarts to work and straighten out this PE thing.

What we told him was that he needed a complete medical workup:

- Like most premature ejaculators (PEs), Germaine needed a full medical exam, a general and sexual history, and special diagnostic testing to understand why this dysfunction was occurring.
- In addition, he might need tests to see how firm an erection he could have. His arteries that supply blood to the penis would also have to be evaluated.
- Sexual counseling might also be necessary to help him learn techniques to delay ejaculation and minimize his shame and embarrassment about this problem.

This sounded too invasive and time-consuming to Germaine. Like a lot of people, he was looking for a shortcut and an instant solution to his problem. There were several drugs that Germaine had heard about and could have tried. For instance, yohimbine is an herbal alternative used to make erections firmer. Methamphetamines have also become very popular with men who have sex with men. People at rave parties or who have "sex weekends" where they have sex repeatedly for days also like "crystal," but Germaine wanted to steer clear of illegal drugs options like that one. Testosterone that enters the body through an implant, patch, injection, or pill was another alternative. Ultimately he chose Viagra, which relaxes blood vessels and allows them to get larger, increasing blood flow, which makes the penis hard.

The first problem with obtaining a drug like Viagra without professional guidance is that it does not work efficiently if certain physical problems need treatment. Viagra is not to be taken by people who take medication containing nitrates. Another problem is that he had no way to know what amount was needed to be effective. Germaine got a supply from the Internet. He had no way to know exactly how much to take. Taking a drug to avoid erectile problems or to sustain erections for long periods of time can also lead to serious addictions. You can get hard but you are hooked on the drug that helps you get an erection.

Germaine was right to take some action on his problem. Unfortunately, he took a shortcut without a medical doctor's advice. Years later he discovered his diabetes.

Jack: How to Tell That Your Partner Needs Treatment

How do you know if the man in your life needs medical help to deal with erection problems? After all, not all erectile problems are unexpected. Some changes in erections are just to be anticipated. As men age and testosterone declines, erections become less frequent. And if orgasm occurs it takes much longer to regain an erection.

Open and honest communication may produce the support necessary to change, get medical help, and improve your sex life and your relationship. Untreated or self-treated illnesses may be disastrous and lead to a gradual loss in desire to have sex at all.

Such was the case for Jack, a Japanese American from San Francisco. He had just celebrated his fiftieth birthday when he learned he had an abnormally low testosterone level caused by a pituitary tumor. He was having problems getting an erection and maintaining his partner's interest in sex. He felt embarrassed even to talk to his girlfriend about his erectile dysfunction. He was worried that he was losing his manliness and would not be able to perform sexually, which made it even harder to try to have sex.

Like most men who have problems with erectile dysfunction, Jack was nervous about what to expect from his sexual performance. He started avoiding foreplay, kissing, hugging, and touching that might get his partner excited. When they did have sex, he placed pressure on her to rush to it.

This was a no-win strategy for both Jack and his partner. Attempting sexual intercourse with a penis that is not fully erect can lead to pain, infection, and frustration for both partners. Repeated attempts to enter the vagina or anus can cause tearing of a woman's skin and tissue. Bacteria or viruses can enter these tears and cause infection that could spread to other parts of the body.

In Jack's case, persuading him to have more communication with his partner was more important than simply providing him with a quick solution. Partners of men with long-term histories of erectile dysfunction will often suffer from low sexual desire themselves even when or if the problems subside. For Jack and his girlfriend, it was important to understand and stop expecting problems. Instead, with medical help, they needed to focus on looking for solutions.

Raheed: When Erectile Dysfunction Is a Side Effect

Erectile dysfunction is also a common side effect of other illnesses, as some men will discover. For example, Raheed is a forty-four-year-old Middle Eastern man with a family history of heart disease. Both his father and older brother had died in their fifties from heart attacks. They had told Raheed about their erectile dysfunction while they were taking heart medication. Now Raheed had high blood pressure. Raheed finally found a pill that kept his blood pressure low and had less of an effect on his ability to get an erection. However, he was afraid that when he became sexually excited he would have a heart attack. He avoided sexual intercourse: when he was infrequently sexually active, he would have anxiety attacks and fears of dying.

Conversations with Raheed centered on his fears. He finally admitted he was so afraid of death that he could not enjoy living. He was physically attractive to women, but his partners never stayed with him long. It was easy to see why. But he used this excuse to explain why he could not find the right woman. He is now in long-term psychotherapy.

There are some sexual problems that just won't go away. You have to understand why they happen in order to keep them from occurring. For example, it is a well-known fact that medicines that control high blood pressure can also cause erectile dysfunction. Among men age forty to seventy years old, erectile dysfunction is as high as 50 percent because of high blood pressure and its treatment. The concerns that Raheed had about physical activity are also common. The good news is that while sexual activity does increase the risk of heart attacks, the risk is very low. The rates do not exceed 1 percent per year in people with active heart disease. While professional help is needed to minimize other problems when a partner is controlling his blood pressure, sex is usually not one of them.

Sally and Jane: Coping with Diabetes

Diabetes is a condition with considerable potential sexual impact, both physical and psychological. The disease is more common in men, but it also affects sexual performance in women. Diabetes can be associated with a loss of desire and arousal. Diabetics may also experience rejection from their partners because people assume that nothing can be done to restore sexual desire and capability. The key to sexual healing with diabetes is understanding how sex factors into it.

Sally, a thirty-something Canadian, successfully hid her diabetes from her partner, Jane. She paid little attention to her diet until her doctor explained that her problem becoming sexually aroused or excited related to her inability to control her blood sugar. Her diabetes had been untreated for so long that her arteries did not allow for the sufficient blood flow needed for lubrication of her vagina.

Sally began to follow a strict diet and exercise plan, but she was reluctant to test her own blood because her partner worked from their home and would notice what she was doing. The doctor suggested that they both come in for the next visit. Sally tearfully told Jane about her condition. Jane was hurt because Sally had kept her diabetes a secret but not because she had an illness.

We discussed how Jane could help Sally test her blood, walk with her, and make her diet a part of their regular eating routine.

"I have diabetes in my family, Sally. I'm the last one to be judgmental. One day, I may have it, too," Jane said.

"Let's test you on a regular basis for diabetes and not wait for any surprises," we advised.

Sally now has her blood sugar under control. Devices like the Eros-CTD, or medications including Intimacy Creme for Women (formerly Viacreme), ProSensual, Zestra for Women, or

ArginMax are available to increase blood flow to the clitoris. There are other trials ongoing to determine if Viagra can increase blood flow to the clitoris. Some of these devices and medications have been successfully used to increase female arousal and orgasm. As we discussed her next steps, Sally seemed a lot more cheerful.

The Power of Talking about Your Health

It's amazing how unhappy hiding the truth from yourself and others can make you. It's even more amazing what a difference medical counseling can make. Talking openly and honestly with a health provider helped Sally to overcome sexual problems that would have affected not only her health but also her relationship. Raheed benefited from counseling about his heart condition and his sexual performance in learning to live with his health problems.

Unfortunately, quality health care is not guaranteed to everyone. Recently, the Institute of Medicine, an independent research group that advises Congress, reported racial disparities in health care even among people with the same insurance. More ethnic minorities died from heart disease and diabetes than whites did. They were less likely to have bypass surgery and more likely to have lower limb amputation. The resulting impact on relationships is significant. Adjusting to the loss of a loved one, lack of access to quality medical care, changes in sexual performance, and the stress of having a chronic illness or disability can significantly affect relationships. Most people often fail to understand the behavior of a partner with a chronic illness and misinterpret silence as disinterest in the relationship.

If you have a chronic disease, you need to talk openly about your illness and advocate for your health care in the medical system. Friends, family, and loved ones can benefit from factual information that you may have learned. Advocating for your health might mean you must do the following:

- Ask your health care provider questions. Be prepared and write questions down between your health visits. Professionals will realize that you know your rights to good medical care and will spend more time with you. If they don't, get the names of supervisors, department chairs, and directors. Write letters documenting that you are not getting the care that you need.

- Take a friend with you and ask them to take notes during your visit. If you have difficulty understanding all of the medical words and how the medications prescribed will affect you, ask the professional to write down the words and the names of the medications. Look up the words in a medical dictionary. On your next visit, ask more questions and use the medical words in your sentences. Your goal is to speak the language of your health provider. Make sure that you have a full understanding of how to describe what is happening to your body.

- Discuss what you have learned about your illness or the medication with your friends, family, and loved ones. You can help to educate them, too.

- If you need to ask sex questions, ask your friend to step out of the room. Information about how your chronic illness is affecting your sex life is private and does not need to be shared with everyone—just the ones who will be affected by your sexual performance.

R_x for Better Sex with Chronic Illness

Chronic illnesses may not go away, but that doesn't necessarily mean you need to end or stop having sex. If you don't expect to function normally, you won't. But if you want sex, it's quite possible to find a way to have it and increase your satisfaction. Try this three-step approach:

Step 1

Ask a medical professional to help you understand more about the illness and how it affects the brain and body. Do your own research in books or on the Internet.

Step 2

Adjust your sexual activity to provide maximum satisfaction in spite of the chronic illness. You may need a trial-and-error period, support from your sex partner, and advice from your health care provider.

Step 3

Focus on honest and direct communication with your partner. The future of your relationship and your sex life may depend on it.

Melinda and Oscar: Coping with Lumps and Bumps

Tumors of all kinds, especially fibroids, can cause painful sex and can complicate becoming pregnant and giving birth. Here are some facts about fibroids that you may not know:

- The chances of miscarriage are greater in women who have fibroid tumors.

- If you have fibroid tumors, you may not have enough blood in your body (a condition called anemia) as a result of heavy vaginal bleeding.
- You may have both bladder and bowel problems caused by pressure from fibroid tumors.
- Fibroid tumors can separate from the uterus and travel to other parts of the abdomen.

These physical problems can affect your interest in sex. The biggest problem is that most people aren't aware of the many problems associated with fibroid tumors and suffer in silence. They risk losing sexual partners, who may be clueless about their problems. Melinda was such a person.

Melinda and Oscar, both twenty-seven, white, and from St. Louis, had been dating for two months without engaging in sexual intercourse. Her primary reason for avoiding sex was fear that it would be as painful as it had been in the past. Her last partner had broken up with her because of this problem. Oscar was persistent and really wanted sexual intercourse. He pressured Melinda to agree to have sex in order to maintain their relationship. As Melinda expected, sex was very painful.

After a long discussion, she agreed to see a doctor, who discovered fibroid tumors. The position of one of the fibroids was close enough to her vagina that Oscar's penis would touch it when they tried to have intercourse. There was good reason for Melinda's pain.

The doctor recommended a myomectomy, a surgical operation to remove the tumors while leaving the uterus intact, and Melinda agreed. But her problems were not over. After surgery, she developed adhesions, or scars, around the uterus and sex was still painful.

Oscar was visibly disappointed.

The Inside Story: What You May Need to Teach Each Other

Melinda and Oscar had very different sexual histories.

- Oscar had a satisfying sex life prior to dating Melinda. Melinda never had painless sex.

- Oscar was orgasm-focused and preferred sexual intercourse. Melinda, uninterested in intercourse, attempted to achieve orgasm through masturbation and oral sex.

- Both partners had never openly and honestly discussed their sexual expectations with each other.

- Melinda had used alcohol to control her pain. Oscar had never used drugs with sex.

- Melinda had talked with friends about sex and their sex lives but had never revealed her own sex problem. Oscar never talked about his sex life and had little understanding about female sexual problems.

They both had a lot to learn. Fortunately, neither Oscar nor Melinda had been sexually or physically abused, which would have complicated their situation. And they were able to communicate openly and honestly about their problems, even though they had never talked about sex with previous partners. After Melinda had her adhesions removed, they began sex therapy.

First, we helped Melinda recognize how much she really cared for Oscar. She learned to set priorities and focus on what really mattered, their relationship. She also learned that sexuality in relationships means more than sexual intercourse. We encouraged Oscar and Melinda to teach each other how they wanted to be kissed, touched, and held, and how they liked to get sexually excited.

Brandon's Story: Living with a Disability

When you become disabled, many different parts of your life can change. Medical disabilities present many challenges to usual sex patterns and relationships. They may create physical barriers to hugging and closeness, a need for assistance, and a loss of privacy. They inevitably require changes in how you and your partner relate to each other.

There are no easy solutions. Each person in the relationship has to find a level of comfort that includes mutual love and intimacy. Unfortunately, many people with disabilities are taken advantage of sexually and not treated with the respect they deserve. Disabled women are abused twice as much as women without physical disabilities. Although deserving to be a sexual partner, a disabled woman may not be regarded as a potential lover.

Disabled men, on the other hand, may find it difficult to bond with men or women. A disability often prohibits the active, independent, tough, and aggressive behavior many men are socialized to believe they must have. Most disabled men know that trying to compete for a partner may be a prescription for failure and another assault on their self-esteem. Such was the case for Brandon.

Brandon came from a family of football players. His father pushed him to play football ever since he could remember, and he was good. He broke all of the city records for rushing and was recruited by many major colleges. He selected a Midwest powerhouse with a football tradition. He started on the varsity team in his freshman year and, by his senior year, he was a Heisman Trophy candidate. He was also doing well in school academically and had dated many of the popular women at his college. He was a hunk and a jock. Greatness was in Brandon's grasp and he could barely wait for the pros.

His team was undefeated and needed one additional win to play for the league championship. On the morning of the last game of the season, Brandon awakened with stomach cramps. He disregarded them. Everything he wanted in life could be showcased in this final college game.

They were leading 32 to 7 with less than five minutes left in the game. The coach motioned for him to let the backup running back finish the game. His team had the ball on the ten-yard line and was poised to score. He asked the coach to let him have one last shot at a touchdown, and the coach left him in the game. On the snap of the ball he ran past the quarterback, receiving the ball as he ran. The opposing tackle and linebacker met him with equal force. As he fell to the ground he thought he heard something snap. As the bodies cleared, he noticed a numbness in his legs and he was unable to stand. He was carried off the field.

Later, Brandon lay motionless on the X-ray table as he saw the radiologist talking to the coach and his dad. The three men approached him with the bad news: a spinal cord injury. He might never be able to walk again. Devastated, he began the long painful rehabilitation process and did not show much improvement in the first six months. For the first time in his life, Brandon experienced fear and despair.

Brandon had reached a crossroad in his life. He had been raised to show no signs of weakness and express anger only in competition. He had played sports all his life where he was able to excel, but he had never been able to express his true feelings and show intimacy or caring. He also had never had to communicate sexually and focus on pleasure and intimacy rather than performance and orgasm. He had paid little attention to anyone other than himself. Now he was grateful that the day nurse, Kristin, was always ready to talk to and nurture him.

As she massaged his legs one morning he took a closer look

and realized how pretty she was. That old feeling suppressed after the injury was awakening, but something was missing. Although he felt tingling in his breast nipples, when she massaged his legs there was no tingling, warmth, or pleasurable sensation in his testicles or penis.

Later that day, he spoke with his doctor about sex and was told he should be able to get an erection and have successful intercourse. He was also told he could have children. Brandon was still puzzled about how his body would work now. The doctor explained his neurological exam revealed Brandon still had pinprick sensation in his penis and scrotum, indicating his nerves were functioning. He could still propel sperm through his penis. Brandon began to feel sexual sensations more frequently in his genitals over the next three months (many people will be able to resume sex in less than a year after a spinal cord injury).

Wanting to become sexually active again, Brandon first called some of his old girlfriends, but they weren't interested in caring for a disabled person for the rest of their lives. Kristin had been aware of Brandon's recent ability to feel sensations again and knew her touch was awakening his sexuality. Brandon had also been aware of Kristin's change in behavior and led the conversation to a different level. Soon they were discussing common likes and dislikes. Brandon was not completely sure, but he felt Kristin liked him and decided to become more assertive in their relationship. He asked Kristin for a kiss and she consented. They found time for privacy to explore each other sexually.

At first it was awkward for Brandon. He needed assistance in moving from one position to another, but Kristin, trained in caring for disabled people, was nonjudgmental, kind, and helpful. After exhausting all forms of petting, Brandon decided it was time to ask Kristin to have sex with him. He was apprehensive but she said "yes." They were both tested for STDs and HIV. They shared their written results and planned the place, time, and date to consummate their love. She was delighted to be "on top" so she could direct his penis where she got the most pleasure.

Brandon was able to get an erection firm enough to penetrate Kristin and ejaculate, even though it was not as intense as before his injury. He was happy again because he had not lost his ability to perform sexually and was grateful for any sexual contact he could have. Although his choices for relationships were now limited, he had found Kristin, a partner more loving than any other woman he had known. Had he not become disabled, he would not have met his life partner. Neither would he have slowed down to experience and appreciate an intimate relationship.

A Compromise

Not all stories of disabled men and women have such fortunate outcomes. Consider José and his family.

One Sunday on their weekly outing, they were involved in a terrible car accident that left José unable to move his arms and legs. Once proud of his body, José became depressed as he saw his muscles waste away. He talked about never again being able to touch or be touched by a woman. His brother and father refused to accept his tearful conclusion.

They pooled their money and found a house where sex workers lived and worked. They interviewed numerous women and investigated their histories before selecting a few that they told about José. Elaina was willing to see him. She agreed to be tested for sexually transmitted diseases and HIV/AIDS. Passing all these tests, they arranged a meeting for José and Elaina.

José's family did not tell him where he was going. They

dressed him and took him to Elaina. She came out and asked José if he would like to have dinner with her. José understood and agreed. Before his father left him, José smiled. Not unlike being left at school for the first time, José was about to learn something new about himself.

Elaina fed José and gave him an erotic massage. She rubbed warm oils all over his body and said sexy things to him. While he was not able to feel everything, watching Elaina lovingly touch his body was just what he needed. José was so at peace that he fell asleep. When he awoke, she called his family and they came for him.

On the ride home, everyone was waiting for a report.

"It's private," José said, interrupting all of the jokes. He had something to dream about for a long time or until his family could arrange another date.

The friendship that Elaina and José developed became more important as time progressed. Their conversations and intimacy formed the basis for a real relationship that José could be proud of.

Remember This Important Clue

Appreciate what you *can* do and the people who are on your side. Make the most of your assets by increasing the quality of the relationships that mean the most to you. Supportive people will help you change your attitude if you let them expect a positive outcome. Just be prepared to work hard to redefine your sexuality to fit the medical disabilities you face.

6

Clueless about Drugs

Secret #6: Drugs that drive what you do drive your relationship, too.

When was the last time you took birth control pills, antidepressants, or other prescription medication? How about the last time you had a drink? These are all drugs that can impact your sex life. So can a variety of designer drugs and other substances, some legal and some not.

So few people know how everyday drug use can change their sex life that this may be one of the most important chapters you will read in this book. Let's begin by looking at a drug that seems harmless in relationships because it is used for good sexual and medical reasons: birth control pills.

Maggie's Choice: The Sexual Side Effects of Contraceptives

Birth control pills aren't always just wonder drugs that make it possible for women to minimize centuries-old fears of unwanted pregnancies. There's a downside that can end up ruining your love life if you don't pay attention.

The fact is that some birth control pills, for all their advantages, also interfere with normal sexual functioning. While you worry less about pregnancy, one of the effects is that your desire for sex may diminish. How does this happen? Birth control pills may lower hormone (testosterone) levels in your body. In other words, pills work in part because they dampen your body's efforts to try to get pregnant.

If you are sexually active, or plan to be, you may be surprised to find that you cannot be as sexually excited as you expected if you are taking birth control pills. That's what happened to Maggie, a twenty-two-year-old New Orleans native. She had been living with her boyfriend, Phillip, for three months when he asked her to take birth control pills so he could stop using condoms. Thinking this was a fair request and being eager to experience sex the way he wanted, she got a six-month supply of birth control pills from her doctor.

It wasn't long before she and Phillip both noticed a decrease in her sex drive. Her doctor prescribed another high-dose birth control pill, but the side effect was the same. Soon she stopped taking the pills. When we first saw Maggie, Phillip was back to using condoms. Now neither of them was sexually satisfied. It took several office visits before Maggie found a low-dose birth control pill that worked for her.

Maggie and her partner understood that they needed to protect each other from pregnancy. By patiently communicating with and supporting each other, they experimented with various methods of contraception that would allow them to enjoy sex responsibly. They both knew that sex was an important, but not primary, basis for love. They valued sexual pleasure in their relationship, but they valued freedom from pregnancy just as much. The trick was to find the balance, and they did.

> ### Remember This Quick Fact
>
> Birth control pills will regulate your menstrual cycle and give you 99.9 percent protection from pregnancy if you take them as instructed. The birth control patch will give the same protection if used correctly. But the patch and birth control pills do not have the same effect on everyone.

The Inside Story on the Pill

While taking birth control pills, some women like Maggie report a decrease in their sex drive, sexual feelings, or sexual nature (libido). Others report an increase or no change.

Pills with high levels of hormones with androgen (testosterone) affect and can actually increase sexual feelings. But women who are not sexually active may find increased interest in sex to be equally undesirable because feeling "horny" can increase tension, nervousness, and anxiety. The bottom line is that your doctor should evaluate your sexual desire along with your sexual history and help you to decide which type of birth control best fits your and your partner's needs.

For your own sake and the sake of your relationship, there are six other important factors to weigh along with the sexual side effects of your contraceptive choices:

1. **"Am I willing to have incurable illnesses or die because I want to have sex with my partner?"** Taking pills to prevent pregnancy does nothing to protect you or your partner against STDs or HIV transmission. The fear of contracting these can decrease your interest in sex and how often you want to have sex. When you worry less about getting a disease as a result of sex, you can enjoy it more. We recommend using condoms for protection against disease even if you are using another form of contraceptive.

2. **"What can happen to my relationship if the pills aren't working out?"** Pills are supposed to reduce worries about unintended pregnancy, but as you have seen in Maggie's story, sometimes they also increase depression and bring on a lethargy or sluggishness that is undesirable. So take signs of mood changes, depression, or lack of interest in sex seriously. If you are less interested in sex or your daily activities because you feel blue or depressed, you may cry easily or be irritable. Your partner may interpret your moodiness as rejection and become more distant or irritable in return. Don't let your partner be the last to know that birth control pills are affecting your moods. You need to talk with him about your medication and its effect on your emotions and your sex drive. Remember, there are many types of birth control methods available today. In a sexual relationship worth keeping, he will understand that you are not the only one responsible for finding a solution.

3. **"What are my chances of getting pregnant?"** With your doctor's advice, select a method of birth control with the highest certainty of preventing pregnancy that does not severely affect your sex drive. Remember, you can't get a little bit pregnant. So if you don't want it to happen, take every measure to make sure that it doesn't.

4. **"Am I ready for sex or pregnancy? Is this someone that I want to share parenting responsibilities with for the rest of my life?"** Just because you may worry less about pregnancy, you should still be very confident that sex at this time in your life and with the person you are considering having sex with is in your best interest.

5. **"Have I asked my partner if he agrees to share parenting responsibilities with me?"** If your answer is "no," you really need to worry about pregnancy. Use a contraceptive method that consistently works for you, no matter what pressures you are under in your relationship to take more chances.

6. **"If this relationship does not last, will I be prepared to raise a child alone?"** If you are not prepared to deal with a mistake or accident, you really shouldn't be risking making one. Discuss your preferred method of birth control with your partner so that both of you are prepared for any outcome, like a pregnancy. Make sure that you are not depending on the strength of the relationship when you should be depending on yourself. If you honestly doubt that you will be able to handle anything that might happen as a consequence of sex with this partner, you need to look for some other outlet for sexual pleasure.

Are You Remaining Silent and Unprotected?

In a study conducted with 900 African American, Latina, and white women, ages eighteen to fifty, African American women were found most likely to make decisions about contraceptive use alone without communicating with their partners. The most common decision made was to use no contraceptive at all. Women who believed that their chances of attracting a partner were contingent on their not bringing up difficult issues, like contraceptive or condom use, remained silent and took their chances.

The numbers of African American and Latina women and poor uneducated women of any race becoming pregnant or infected with STDs or HIV are great and increasing. It's up to you not to become a statistic.

Bill's Dilemma: Dealing with the Side Effects of Antidepressants

There is no question that medications such as antidepressants have increased the quality of many lives. But antidepressants that change the chemical imbalance in your brain can also affect the rest of your body. The antidepressant drugs known as selective serotonin reuptake inhibitors (SSRIs) in particular are associated with side effects that alter sexual desire and performance and therefore affect relationships. These drugs can decrease your interest in sex, your ability to have an orgasm, and your sexual satisfaction.

If a woman has low sexual desire because she is depressed, SSRIs can make matters even worse. Antidepressants can also affect men experiencing difficulty in getting and retaining an erection. This is what happened to Bill.

Born in Butte, Montana, Bill was thirty years old and severely depressed. When we first met him, he had recently lost his best friend in an auto accident that he survived. After the accident, he was immediately placed on a common antidepressant. He felt less depressed, but he was no longer interested in sex at all and his wife didn't understand why. She feared losing the physical elements of their relationship at the same time that they were struggling with the emotional parts. Intuitively, she knew that would lead to the slow death of their marriage.

Bill stopped taking his medicine in an effort to reignite his sex life and please his wife. Unfortunately, like 40 percent of people who discontinue this medication, he again became severely depressed, and his sexual dysfunction continued.

This story would have had a very unhappy ending if Bill had hidden the reason for halting his medication from his doctor. But because he openly shared that information, his doctor was able to change his prescription so that Bill's sexual side effects were less severe. Ultimately, Bill began to feel less guilty about the accident. He was able to appreciate that his survival was a blessing and not a curse. He took daily walks with his wife. With the resulting increase in his blood flow, along with a healthy diet that prohibited smoking or drinking, he found his sex drive returning and his wife, delighted.

Get a Clue

Talk to your doctor about how antidepressants are affecting you. Diet, exercise, and sex therapy may be all you need to develop a balance between how well you function sexually and psychologically. But it can be quite challenging to stay sexually active while using drugs for depression.

Adriana's Deception: The Effects of Date Rape Drugs

For a long time, there have been pharmacies of drugs available for people who wanted to make their bodies do more than they were meant for sexually. Barbiturates, inhalants, hallucinogens, cocaine, and PCP are still common choices thought by some to heighten and exaggerate sexual thrills.

Recently, however, "designer drugs," "club drugs," and "date rape" drugs have also caught public attention. Popular designer drugs include ecstasy, gamma hydroxybutyrate (GHB), Rohypnol, ketamine, herbal ecstasy (ma huang, ephedra), and methamphetamines.

It is hardly a coincidence when drugs have sexy names. For example, "liquid ecstasy," "grievous bodily harm," and "scoop" are the street names for GHB. Bodybuilders have used it to stimulate muscle growth. It is an odorless, colorless powder or liquid that, when taken with alcohol, lowers inhibition and produces amnesia within fifteen minutes.

Many of these drugs are used on unsuspecting women and men to increase their sexual performance and to reduce their inhibitions to literally any kind of sexual activity. That's what happened to Adriana.

This seventeen-year-old blond and blue-eyed high school cheerleader found herself in the middle of a nightmare one night. She and her girlfriend had been "selected among finalists" to attend a party to launch a new CD. The girls were thrilled to receive so much attention and assumed that their youth and beauty were the main attraction. Actually, their looks were not exceptional but their naiveté was.

The party was hot and alive with dancing, drinking, and drugs, the three "D's." Adriana met Oliver, a perfectly gorgeous hunk, who quickly explained why he was in a wheelchair. He was healing, he said, from a motorcycle accident.

Oliver and Adriana seemed to hit it off immediately and spent most of the evening talking and drinking. At about midnight Adriana noticed she was slurring her speech and walking with a wobble. Oliver, complaining he needed a pain pill, asked Adriana if she would wheel him to his place and return to the party. Adriana agreed.

She remembers entering Oliver's apartment but nothing else until the next morning. She awoke in bed with Oliver who said she had agreed to have sex with him. While she got dressed, she noticed that Oliver got up and walked without using his wheelchair.

Adriana went home and immediately told her mother what had happened. Her mother did the right thing. She took her to the emergency room. Adriana's urine tested positive for Rohypnol. "Roofies," "rope," or the "forget pill," as Rohypnol is called, is used in anesthesia in several countries but is not marketed in the United States or Canada. When dissolved in a drink, Rohypnol is odorless and tasteless and readily absorbed in thirty minutes. It produces symptoms similar to alcohol intoxication and amnesia.

With support from her mother and the semen that was collected for evidence when she was examined, Adriana had Oliver arrested for rape. She spent the next two years in therapy confronting her fears of men and particularly good-looking ones who seemed harmless.

Unfortunately, Adriana's fears had a basis in reality. There are men who specialize in controlling women for sex. These men have a script. With a prop, like a wheelchair, to draw attention and decrease suspicion of predatory behavior, they then use drugs to get what they want. It's a cheap, cruel method of getting sex without expending effort or money on dating. While appearing attractive and outgoing, in reality, these guys can be very aggressive.

Watch Out for Inhalants

We need to mention a related hazard at this point. There is a growing trend among twelve- to seventeen-year-olds to sniff glue or inhale a variety of noxious chemicals, including paint thinners, gasoline, lighter fluid, spray paint, and others. While these inhalants offer a short-term buzz or high, they can also cause brain damage, memory lapses, and problems with the ability to concentrate. These chemicals also increase the vulnerability of the inhaler to be raped. Well over 2 million youths have sniffed or "huffed" at least once.

Relationships with Drug Users

Consenting relationships that include drug use usually don't last because it's the drug that is in control and not the other way around. But some women don't seem to realize that their partner is a drug user until after they fall in love. Kathy's story comes to mind.

The day we first met Kathy, she was with her boyfriend, Greg. He'd brought her to get treated for a sexually transmitted disease. Kathy was visibly upset.

"Greg was having sex with other people," she mentioned as casually as she could. As it turned out, Greg admitted he was having sex with sex workers (prostitutes) and using street drugs to make women more vulnerable to sexual assault. He had contracted an STD, which he gave to Kathy. It was not the first time. Kathy had decided to stay in the relationship even though she continued to contract STDs. Although she needed to decide where her relationship was going, she still wasn't ready to change or let go of Greg.

If you have a relationship like this, ask yourself:

- What am I getting out of the relationship?
- What am I not getting?
- Does my partner love me?
- Do I have to risk my health?

Sooner or later reality will set in and you will have to come to grips with the fact that you are in a relationship with a drug rather than a person.

Phillip's Story: When Therapy Is the Answer

People tend to believe that drugs enhance sex. However, in the long run, the more you use drugs, the less likely you are to enjoy sex. For example, it took Phillip, a twenty-two-year-old Chinese drug dealer, a year to admit that he was an addict and longer to admit that he was no longer able to sustain an erection. Instead of confronting this problem, he became accustomed to medicating and ignoring his feelings.

When Phillip came to us for therapy, he said it was to deal with his anger at his parents. It took months of being confronted about inconsistent details of his past for him to finally admit his drug use and sexual problem.

He made no attempt to glorify the sordid details. He and his girlfriend used crack cocaine and he sold it to pay for college and their habit. He described wild bouts of sex when they first got together, especially when he rubbed cocaine on the tip of his penis and on the lips of her vagina and clitoris. If their sex was mind blowing, it didn't take long for the effects to require more and more of the drug to get their bodies to work. After a while they would just get high, but neither really could keep track of what happened during sex. He argued that it did not really matter how long he lasted sexually.

"Then why are you here?"

Phillip fearfully told us the truth. For the first time he admitted how deeply he wanted help. Together, we reserved a space for him in a rehab program. He was advised not to have sex or see his girlfriend until he was clean. While his partner was also encouraged to get help with her addiction, her recovery would have to be her responsibility.

What about you? If you are considering this question seriously, you also need to know that there is no therapy that can compete with a drug. If you decide that you want a life without drugs, call for a sex therapy appointment when you are

115

clean. Work on your sexual problem when your drug problem is under control.

Angela's Story: Are You Dealing with Alcohol, or Is It Consuming You?

Many people use alcohol to get ready for sex or to relax. But how many times has sex played second fiddle to your drinking? Blood alcohol levels of 0.4 percent are usually considered toxic and can be easily reached with a glass or two of wine. With this much alcohol in your bloodstream, your coordination, attention, memory, and judgement about sex can be impaired.

And here's a startling fact: alcohol is involved in more than 60 percent of sexual assaults.

Where alcohol is concerned, it is easy to be your own worst enemy. For a while, Angela certainly was. With two married children, she was retired from her secretarial job and long divorced. She had nothing important to do. Her days were filled with playing bridge.

Angela played best while "knockin' 'em back" with her drinking buddies, so her children encouraged her to attend Alcoholics Anonymous meetings. There she met Sam, age sixty, and widowed. They bonded quickly and spent time before and after class talking. They made a bet with each other to see who would stop drinking first and stay sober the longest. Now Angela had a goal for the first time in years. She had always remembered something that her daughter had said.

"It isn't age that stops you from playing and having fun, it's when you stop playing and having fun that you age."

Angela was starting to feel alive again. She began to fantasize about sex with Sam and finally asked him if he was interested. He was, but he had so many years of alcohol abuse and abstinence, he often had erectile problems. However, he refused to get help because of his pride. Neither Angela nor Sam could claim that their desire was as strong as they remembered it to be. It took longer for both of them to become sexually excited. Sam liked to watch porno flicks to get "ready," but Angela told him that he might as well have sex with one of those women in the movies. She did not like to watch him get excited by watching someone else.

Angela noticed how Sam would pick fights with her so he could retreat into one of the bedrooms and watch his porno movies. Sex for him had become more of a spectator sport, a pattern that he did not want to break. Sam also had trouble talking about his past relationships with his wife and children. He had experienced a lot of pain, but he just could not share it. Angela found herself returning to her bridge group to fill her time. One evening when she came home, Sam had a drink in his hand.

"Would you like for me to pour you one?" he asked.

Angela, somewhat distraught over what she knew would not be one drink, answered, "Yes. Let's have a good time. I want to feel young again."

You can guess what happened to Angela. Her recovery from alcohol abuse was dependent on Sam, whom she used to fill her lonely hours and set goals of recovery with. But no relationship by itself can redefine who you are as a person or compensate for past failed relationships and other problems in your life. Developing a relationship with someone who has the same problems and methods of coping that you do is like looking into a mirror and seeing yourself. When you make a wrong move, so does the mirror image.

This was not a good relationship for Angela or Sam. Angela was working against her recovery by being with someone who was resistant to change.

Reality Check

We are not absolutely against drugs. Prescribed drugs can do wonders, and by using a limited amount of alcohol you probably feel sexier. You might feel freer of the frustrations you've experienced in the past, or more comfortable using suggestive body language that signals your interest in sex. But just don't kid yourself. Drugs or alcohol will create more problems in your sex life and in your relationships than they will solve.

Here are three questions to ask yourself if you suspect that drugs and alcohol are a liability in your relationships.

1. **"Do I love myself enough to take control of my body in healthy ways?"** If you think you might need professional help to deal with this question, why not get it? Your life may depend on it.

2. **"Could prescription drugs be a factor in my sexual performance and desire?"** If you take prescribed drugs, find out the realistic benefits and sexual limitations you can expect. Ask your doctor or do some research for yourself in books or on the Internet.

3. **"Does my partner have a problem with drugs or alcohol?"** You may need to get professional help from someone with experience in drug and alcohol recovery to answer this question. Are you a good lover when you use drugs or alcohol? If your partner is using them, how will you ever really know?

7

Clueless Pain

Secret #7: You don't have to be hurt to be loved.

Many people feel they don't deserve sexual gratification unless it comes with pain or great risk. Sexual relationships based on that psychological pattern are more common than you might think. People who like pain inflicted on them—and those who like to administer it—usually don't discuss their preferences in public. Nor do people who need risky thrills to be satisfied. Instead, they have a close circle of like-minded friends. Sometimes these relationships based on risk work. But frequently they're toxic, particularly when they center on extreme drugs or sadomasochistic (S and M) sex games.

Many of the behaviors you'll read about in this chapter are called "games," but they are actually compulsive, self-destructive sexual patterns.

Lee: The Dominatrix

"S and M" games are acted out in real human relationships. One partner plays the slave, student, or bottom and the other is the master, teacher, or top. Other fantasy characters include the dominatrix. Also know as the domme, goddess, or mistress, she is one of the most popular S and M characters.

Lee, a self-assured, twenty-something British expatriate, allowed us to interview her. She said that she had never intended to stay in business so long as a dominatrix, but she had a well-established, highly visible clientele who paid her up to $5,000 per session for her skills and for her silence. Her law degree helped her to stay out of legal trouble, but she only worked a few days a week and made more money than any of her workaholic classmates.

"I wear a long leather coat over a sexy bodysuit, but I am a lot more strict and unforgiving than most mistresses. Most of my clients masturbate, but only after I give them permission. By the time I let them touch themselves, they are begging for mercy. But they love me to be strict: to be their mother, whose approval they had to work so hard for; their teacher who really turned them on when they were paddled at school; their priest who lusted for them but made them recite a thousand 'Hail Marys.'

"Many of my clients were raised in strict and unloving families or sent to boarding schools or religious schools that believed in spanking or punishing children for the slightest infraction. One of my favorite clients used to be made to take down his underwear and bend over the principal's knee when he failed to do his homework. The room was cold and he would get an erection while being spanked. I'm sure that the principal enjoyed this as much as my client learned to. So, he bends over my knee and I spank him. He even tells me what to say.

I have a script and a costume that is exactly like what the principal wore. I begin by just stroking his bottom and then spanking until it hurts but I don't bruise or break the skin. He gets a rock-hard erection and I finally give him permission to release himself [masturbate]. We've been playing these games every two weeks for almost six years.

"I must admit, I get off, too, when he begs me to let him touch himself. Once he was hospitalized and I went to his room and we played our game. I really miss him when he is out of the country. When he's away, we have phone sex or cybersex. He's a compulsive masochist and he met his match with me.

"I believe in S and M," Lee continued. "It can be a very healing and helpful, depending on how it is used. People need to talk extensively about what they are going to do before the games begin, though. That is one of the things, among many, that differentiates sex games from abuse. The partners are willing to do what we do because each time we role-play, the client is working through his abuse and turning it into something positive.

"Wives or partners don't do what I do, so my clients come to a professional mistress. I mean, in an ideal world, my clients would be honest with their wife or their partner and get their needs met in their relationships. If they come to me, I don't see that as a bad thing because at least they are able to maintain their relationship with the person they are with, even if they are not fully honest.

"I do something called play piercing. Play piercing is when you use very small-gauge, fine-tip needles. I sterilize the area and I pierce through a little bit of skin in the genital region, and put it completely through. I am also into cock and ball torture, which involves me putting on latex gloves and placing someone's penis and balls in some kind of intricate little bondage. I handcuff my clients in a chair and then do some light slapping with a crop. Men really like this."

"When you are with your partner, what do you like to have done to you?" we asked during the interview.

She replied: "Personally, I don't like pain at all. I like a little bit of spanking every once in a while, but that is not painful to me, it's arousing. Ever since I was a little girl, I played games where I locked my friends in the closet. I remember playing nun school with one of my Catholic friends. We'd get naked, put skirts on our heads like the nuns' headgear, and beat our dolls! I don't know if I could connect that to what I do now, but I had fantasies when I was child about being a prostitute.

"When I was little, my father used to hurt me. He made me do things and I used to beg him to stop. He never did and the more I begged, the more he would hurt me. I swore that when I grew up, I would never let anyone make me beg again. When I am Mistress Lee, I am so different than I am in my private life. Mistress Lee never lets anyone hurt her—she inflicts the pain. I figure that if I keep working on being able to control my partners, as well as my clients, I won't get hurt anymore."

The Inside Story

This narrative has introduced you to Lee, the person, not just the character. In private, she revealed how her game playing started years ago. Some of the games that she plays with clients were played with her as the victim during her childhood. Being a mistress seems the perfect way for her to act out these childhood scenes again, only this time, she wins.

In reality, however, she is once again the loser. Her bravado masks a lot of emotional pain. When a person experiences painful and traumatic sexual or physical childhood abuse and reenacts those events without the guidance of a mental health professional, high levels of fear, terror, anxiety, stress, or panic return. Paniclike symptoms can include sweating, a dry mouth, stomach pain, and headaches. Lee endures and even welcomes the chance to relive intense sexual arousal despite these symptoms. She can't "work through the pain" and simply experience sexual pleasure without them.

The closer people like Lee hold on to their pain, the more unsatisfactory the results. Experiencing or inflicting pain alone does not cure anyone of what pain represents for them. Survivors of abuse often blame themselves. It is difficult for children or adults to imagine that someone like a family member could punish or hurt them if they were not bad, stupid, clumsy, sexually provocative, or deserving of harm.

This line of thinking reinforces insecurities, especially if seeking pain for gain leads to pleasure, and sexual arousal coincides with sexual or physical abuse. There is such a thin line between pain and pleasure that some people need well-trained professional help even to understand the difference.

Not surprisingly, Lee was still struggling to regain control of sex in her adult personal life. If you relate to her struggle and are truly ready to begin your own transformation, good professional help is essential for you, too.

Therapy can be a life-giving, life-sustaining act. We believe it's a matter of life and death for you to learn to communicate your sexual needs to partners who will hug you and not hurt you. If you don't know how, let a professional talk with you. Learn how to experience pleasure without pain. People with this high-risk pattern frequently show up in emergency rooms. We have had to extract all sorts of devices from vaginas or rectums as a result of women or men letting a game go too far. There are no safeguards when you agree to allow others to take control of your body.

In the meantime, if you do play these games and have a medical condition or take medication, don't count on friends or partners to modify a sex game in order to minimize risks to you. Prior to participating in any games, have a full medical exam and a consultation with your health professional about any medical conditions you have that might put you at risk, such as back or heart problems.

For the same reasons, do a background check on your partner, and have a plan for emergency calls in case of an accident. If you feel uncomfortable about what you are asked to do, don't do it.

Rob's Decision: A Matter of Self-Esteem

Not everyone who seeks and endures painful, destructive sexual relationships has a sadomasochistic motive. Rob, a forty-something gay man from Miami, openly shared his sexual relationship problems with us when he decided to come for therapy. Being gay was an important aspect of his crisis, but not the only cause.

"While there are parts of America and the world where being gay does not mean what it used to twenty years ago, homosexuality is still not universally accepted. For many gay men, there is still a tremendous need for self-acceptance and unconditional love from others."

Rob shared his thoughts with us. "Being gay contradicts everything that I was raised to think about how men are supposed to act. Asking or begging for acceptance makes me feel weak, needy, and far too vulnerable. It's much easier to receive confirmation through sex. You feel good, wanted, powerful, sexy, and, sometimes, loved. I have learned it is important for me to feel loved and accepted.

"You know, this is the first time in my life that I have been alone. I have been in a continuous relationship since I left home. However, no matter how my partners harmed me, I was willing to endure a great deal because I thought that ultimately I would receive the love and acceptance that I needed. Because

I had not come to grips with being gay and I didn't feel good about myself, I would overlook someone who loved me and wanted to settle down and seek out someone who would cause me tremendous pain. I thought *their* life style was much more exciting and I needed to be accepted. My low self-worth made me think I deserved nothing better and I would seek love where I could not possibly find it.

"When I met Sam, my last partner, I was in a long-term relationship with someone who really loved me, but I left him because Sam and I had so much chemistry together. He was exciting and liked to have fun. What's the point of being a 'gay' man if you don't have fun, right? That's the argument I used, and off into a perfectly destructive relationship I went.

"You know, I tried to see Sam on the side for a while, but I felt terrible about violating my promise of monogamy. Actually, I felt less worthy of a faithful partner when I had cheated a few times, so leaving him was my way of 'making myself feel better and not cheating anymore.' It took a while to realize that I was cheating myself and the values that I now know are a part of who I am. My old partner was devastated, but I never looked back. Not until much later, when I, too, was devastated.

"My old partner liked to talk about feelings, which is something that I always had a hard time doing. Sam, well, he wasn't much for words. He liked sex and so did I. It was lights out and no conversation—just fun.

"Sam just didn't like excitement, he craved it. He introduced me to 'crystal' [crystal methamphetamine] so we could have fun for longer periods of time. Before Sam, I had smoked a lot of pot but had been clean for a while. Sam and I started with pot but crystal made me feel so excited, so sexy, and so free. One thing led to another, and we were into sex parties, love parties, and orgies.

"We used to go on the Web and look for parties, scan in our pictures, and wait to see if we were invited or not. One night, we dropped 'ecstasy.' Wow, that was wild. Ecstasy led us to bathhouses. I was scared to be in there because you couldn't see, but I guess that was the point. But the fear and excitement, plus the fact that this was a public place, made the sex so much better. I was hooked on Sam, drugs, sex, and taking risks. We would take Valium at night and go to work the next day. When I could, I started to 'tweak'—I was one of those people who stay up partying for days taking drugs.

"Sam's addiction was really getting out of control. The more drugs he took, so did I. I felt really bad sometimes about what I was doing, but the drugs would make me forget my troubles and have a good time. That was until Sam started to get really paranoid and had to be hospitalized.

"It wasn't long before I started to feel sick. I got a cold that I could not get rid of. I went to the doctor, got tested for HIV, and could not believe the results. I was HIV positive. I don't exactly know why I did not believe that I could be positive, because I knew how people got infected. I was just so busy keeping up with Sam, I didn't really think that it could happen to me.

"I knew that I had to make a decision about my relationship with Sam. It had been two years and I had just about destroyed everything that I owned and pulled away from everyone important to me. I thought that if I stayed with Sam, he could give me the acceptance that I needed. I finally got into counseling to sort things out.

"I learned that my negative feelings about myself began much earlier than when I 'came out.' I had never thought much of myself, so it was easy to be attracted to partners who would confirm that. In order for me to seek partners who will not hurt me or cause me pain, I first have to get to know me and love myself.

"I realize now that one day I will want to be in a relationship again, but not now. I need to be good to myself and know who I am and who I need in my life. I have begun to set boundaries for my self-protection that no one can violate. I don't need to be hurt to be loved. Until I am sure of this, I can't be good for anyone else."

Is It Worth It?

Living teaches us that people have to experience some pain to know what pleasure is. We all have our little hurts and big hurts. We also have to experience some pain to know when we have had too much. We may end up selecting some wrong partners before we appreciate the right ones. We have to be willing to lose a few things to gain others. But that's as far as we go. Past that threshold, we will not tolerate unhappiness, rejection, taking risks, and abuse. It's not a worthy sacrifice, even if we don't get the love that we want.

If someone is causing you pain, what kind of love is that? Both Lee and Rob wanted acceptance, sexual pleasure, and love, but what they got instead was addiction, disease, and pain that compromised their personal growth. Fortunately, Rob discovered the limit of his pain tolerance.

Like Rob, the more you know yourself, the easier it is to say "I've had enough." Without a sense of your pain tolerance, you can easily destroy the quality of life that you actually want and deserve. Sooner or later, you won't be able to recognize and appreciate the peace and contentment that may ultimately feel a lot better than the painful pleasures that you've gotten used to.

Don't be afraid to stop having sex if you see that your behavior can't lead to anything good and healthy in the long run. It's better to have no relationships at all until the decisions you make about sex reflect how you want to be remembered for the rest of your life.

It is your God-given right to insist on pleasure without pain or fear. Settle for nothing less.

R$_X$ for Healing

Ask yourself these questions:

- Do you have past experiences where you have encountered pain and pleasure at the same time?

- Are you reliving these experiences in an effort to overcome or "get over" them?

- Do you have a history of being sexually abused where someone touched or penetrated your body with their mouth, hand, penis, or anything else against your will?

- Have you ever been hit, kicked, punched, or threatened with words or a weapon?

If you answered *Yes* to any of these questions, sex games may be very harmful for you. If you participate in these games to relive the experience, you may only be traumatizing yourself needlessly and increasing feelings of shame, guilt, and low self-esteem. Look for a professionally trained mental health professional with expertise in dealing with trauma to help you in the course of self-discovery.

The following thoughts will give you a head start:

- **Focus on the negative events that occurred in your sexual history and on healing the pain you experienced then.** An experienced professional should help you see why you keep returning to unhealthy relationships. It is not sex that should be the focus of your healing, but how you feel about past abuses or trauma.

- **How does your body respond automatically to certain stimuli or sexual practices?** Remember, your body responds sexually because usually your brain has signaled it to do so. If you want to change, learn how to control your response to painful or traumatic sexual stimuli. Avoid blaming yourself if your body responded in unacceptable ways to someone who hurt you in the past. Don't feel compelled to punish yourself more if you don't like the way you behaved sexually.

- **Are your orgasms more intense, especially if you deprive or degrade yourself or experience discomfort, fear, or pain?** Being in control of your sexuality is as important as being able to experience sexual pleasure. What arouses you makes an important personal statement about who you are, so you need help to be selective. Sexual arousal is controllable, and no one should control it but you.

- **Are you convincing yourself that the decisions you are making about sex are the best ones?** No sexual partner whom you pay or control will ever take responsibility for telling you the truth. You need someone else to help you take an objective look at your script for risky relationships.

- **What do your friends and family say about your behavior?** If you have no outside feedback about your sexual activities other than people who are practicing the same behaviors, you are too isolated. Ask a trusted friend, a therapist, or someone you respect to tell you what they think about your behavior and your relationships. Be prepared to really listen. Sometimes we don't want to hear what others will say and we avoid these open conversations, but we need to know. Changing any relationship begins with changing certain behavior. Only *you* can change your behavior.

8

Clueless Victims

Secret #8: Predators know your weaknesses.

On any given day in the wild, predators stalk their prey. Stronger animals overpower the weaker ones and bring them to a swift end. Human sexual predators are no different. Some seek out victims who are seemingly helpless to resist them. Others prey on people who are looking for love, acceptance, and someone to trust. They quickly spot weaknesses in their prey and make a plan to take advantage of them. The fact that predators use all of their skills and energy to take control of others can leave their victims clueless about why they were selected as prey and how they can escape a predator's grasp.

People who use relationships for sexual conquests do so in different ways and to varying degrees. The range runs the gamut, including:

1. Taking casual advantage of others' weaknesses
2. Rape
3. Practicing the skills of aggression in an inappropriate way or on an inappropriate target
4. Preying on children and young teenagers

Predators can be outlaws in society. But more often than not, the predators who can pose the greatest threat to most women are the kind of men society lifts up as its role models and heroes. Ironically, these men are well paid and honored for their ability to take control. Trained to fight, intimidate, or use physical or verbal confrontation to get their way, they may be:

- Athletes
- Soldiers
- Policemen and bodyguards
- Businessmen
- Attorneys
- Boxers or wrestlers

Predators exist in every profession, and every once in a while, they're women. The main thing to know about them is that they are connoisseurs of sexual scripts that expose your vulnerability.

Saman's Script: Caught on a Summer Night

We were at an outdoor music festival one summer, and the mood was festive and friendly. Saman, a pretty, twenty-something, curly-haired woman chatted with us momentarily, as she swayed closer to the stage. Her round eyes were glassy and fixed as she inhaled the smells that filled the night air.

Saman wore a tight-fitting blouse that revealed more than her shoulders. Her skirt showed every movement of her behind and thighs. As she danced slowly to the music, Saman was something to see. But that's what she wanted—she was "catching" or looking for love. The crowd thinned, leaving her even more conspicuous. The music stopped for a moment, but Saman continued her suggestive dance. As she closed her eyes and drank more wine, the music began again.

That's when the stranger made his move. Silently, he slid up behind her, moving his body in sync with hers. He offered to help her take photos and refilled her empty glass. He placed his hands on her hips to guide their syncopated movements. Whispering in her ear, he lightly brushed the back of her neck. She blushed and half-heartedly resisted, obviously pleased with

Remember This Clue

The nicest people go to these places, but so do the strangest people. Be wary of letting your sexual guard down at:

- Concerts
- Church
- Gyms
- Bars
- Coffee houses
- Nightclubs
- Restaurants
- Sports events
- Libraries
- Museums
- Schools
- College and university events

her catch. He was very focused and was not about to be distracted. He grabbed her hand and managed a gentle kiss as he pulled her into his seat. Soon their legs were locked in an embrace. His hands moved along her thighs as he soothed her with his words. As the music grew louder, he lifted her to her feet and pulled her close for a long passionate kiss. Saman resisted no longer. He grabbed her hand, pulled her up the aisle, and they disappeared into the crowd.

The Inside Story

Predators like Saman's will read your script and exploit it for sexual conquest. They favor public settings where, if confronted or rejected, they can quickly get lost in the crowd and look for someone else to "hit on." They often travel to events with friends who engage in the same behavior and share stories of their exploits.

Mac's Script: "Filling That Empty Space"

Predators who like to control their prey don't easily give up. They are relentless in their pursuit because of the thrill of the conquest, not because they have genuine feelings or concern for anyone other than themselves.

Mac's success was based on his ability to find women to exploit. "They have a look," he said.

At age thirty-two, dressed to the nines, Mac considered himself "right about the game," as a good pimp. In our interview, he openly admitted exploiting "bitches and ho's," as he called them. He liked to "turn out" a woman by having sex with her and making her get "on the track" for him. Out of respect, he said, his three ho's had sex with him and took care of his every need. He felt he made life easier for them by managing their money.

"They have titties and booties but no brains and usually get their money all f—— up. If they get arrested, I bail them out. I protect them, but I don't love 'em. Love don't mix with this business. Most of 'em come from homes where nobody cares about 'em or they were abused or beat up all the time. When they work for me, I fill that empty space in their lives.

"Sometimes, when they don't respect me, I have to hit 'em up-side their heads, but it's okay. They're used to it. It's called knockin'. They straighten up after that. Besides, some of 'em think you don't love 'em if you don't hit 'em. When they work for me, I have to recondition their minds. They do what I tell 'em."

In order to maintain control, Mac often uses verbal abuse to demean and humiliate women. He also favors physical force, like hitting, kicking, punching, or threatening to harm or kill their pets, and to control or minimize resistance to his demands. Overpowering with words is so effective that women will eventually internalize his power and comply with his demands with few words spoken.

Some predators only have to glance before women willingly submit to their control. Mac beat the women who prostituted for him.

"Don't make me have to come over there" was all he had to say. He'd finish a beating with "See what you made me do?" Predators rarely accept responsibility for hurting others but make no mistake—they enjoy it.

Too Little, Too Much, Too Soon

Predators are experts on how to prey on others but clueless about how to be in a mutually loving relationship. What they know, they learned young, and it easily becomes a lifelong habit.

At a juvenile detention center in the Midwest, we met Miguel, a charming seventeen-year-old detainee from Cuba. Fearing that he might be detained for more crimes, Miguel told us about his friend, Peter, who fits this description of a predator perfectly.

Peter, the seventh of ten children, grew up very poor and alone in Cuba. His parents could not care for him and asked his uncle, an alcoholic, to raise him. His uncle would take him to bars and made him wait while he had sex with prostitutes or women who had too much to drink. Peter's job was to make sure that his uncle got home safely. Sometimes Peter's uncle would use him for sex. He would fondle Peter's genitals or make him perform oral sex. When Peter resisted, his uncle would beat him. Peter had little time to be around other kids. He was always in the principal's office because he would come to school late after a night out with his uncle. Eventually, he dropped out of school.

You can say that Peter honed his skills as a rapist from imitating his uncle's behavior. He learned to "numb out," or dissociate his feelings, as a result of his own sexual and physical abuse. So, whenever he had sex, he didn't really feel anything. In fact, most of the time, he could not sustain an erection. What he did feel was power. His uncle would sometimes rape a prostitute and let Peter rape her, too. They would laugh and drink together, bragging about their conquests.

One night, Peter's uncle got into a fight with several men who had been drinking and bled to death while Peter ran for help. At age thirteen, Peter was living on the street, "turning tricks" or prostituting, and was using drugs. One of the dealers asked him to bring some drugs into the United States and that's how he got to Miami.

Peter had never had a sexual experience that did not involve money or violence so he resorted to his old habits: he

> ## Remember This Clue
>
> Before the age of eighteen, one out of every three women and one out of every four to five men will be raped. While the majority of rapists are male, growing numbers of females are being incarcerated for sexual assaults and for raping other females and males.
>
> Rape is a violation of your body, against your will. This is an experience that you can't overlook once it enters your sexual history. Surviving rape has severe effects on your sense of self-control, the ability to protect yourself, and your belief that you can control your own body and your life.

started picking up women again. He would accompany them home or follow them, break in, and rape them. Once the police got too suspicious of him, he would move to another city. He was finally caught at age seventeen. He had raped nearly fifty women since he was ten years old.

Barry's Script: No Boundaries between Bedroom and Boardroom

Predators who are trained and reinforced for their aggression are often attractive but clueless about why their personal lives do not work for them, given their other material success. They can have all the sex they want because they seem to be desirable partners. But it is unrealistic to expect predators to give up any control or display of their aggression to get what you want—unconditional love, trust, and respect.

Barry's story is typical. One night his chauffeur brought

the car around, picked up Barry and his assistant, and took them to the private airstrip where he boarded his plane for Russia. This thirty-seven-year-old attorney had everything to gain on this deal and had invested millions making sure that it would go through.

He arrived in the evening. He had a set pre-meeting agenda when the stakes of the business deal were high—as they were in this case. It included sex with a young prostitute whom he treated so roughly that she later required medical treatment for bleeding from her vagina and rectum. "Rough sex" made Barry feel superior, and totally in control, just what he felt he needed before a tough business negotiation.

When men like Barry practice aggression daily in the workplace, they can become convinced that all success depends on their cunning ability to overwhelm, intimidate, and harm others. This work style often spills over into their private lives. One quickly gets the impression that they think they are special and should be allowed to behave differently than others. Their work and social status often leads them to assume that they should be protected from prosecution. For sex, they prey on what they consider to be "throwaway people."

Young, poor, recently immigrated, drug-addicted, and isolated people with no one to protect them are favorite targets of men like Barry. So, too, are their wives and girlfriends.

Test Your Relationship

Ask yourself these questions. Do your sexual relationships reflect:

- **Too much control of one partner over the other, sometimes with very severe consequences?** Physical or sexual abuse often occurs if the passive partner violates the rules of the predator.

- **The same rules that exist in business are sometimes applied to personal relationships?** Predators often do not develop alternative methods of listening, reasoning, negotiating, or attempting to compromise over conflicts.

- **Very immature styles of problem solving?** Predators have an "If I can't get my way, I will leave or you have got to go" mentality. This kind of attitude often results in affairs, short-term relationships, or marriages with multiple children.

- **Partner shopping?** Predators commonly stay with one person, have children (perhaps), get bored, leave, and find someone else. All of the people in a predator's world are expected to live by the predator's rules.

- **The partner being tolerated for money or status?** The chances of having real friendships or relationships that do not involve power and control simply elude men like Barry.

Remember This Clue

Some predators experience sexual pleasure, arousal, and satisfaction with children. Pedophiles are often difficult to identify because they are usually so well integrated into our society. They are friendly to children and adults, and are usually involved in children's activities. They are skilled in finding opportunities to be alone with children who are isolated, lonely, and not emotionally close to their families. Pedophiles need intensive psychotherapy and a structured environment to live in to help them understand their behavior and to protect others from them.

Can They Change?

There are many people who don't realize they are predators and, even worse, while exhibiting predatorlike behavior, are in total denial. If you, your partner, and others in your life are affected by predatory behavior, you will benefit from seeing a trained therapist for help.

Think about how your partner expresses his or her sexuality. Do you have a partner who:

- Consistently takes advantage of other people's weaknesses to have sex?
- Looks at child pornography on a regular basis?
- Has problems resisting being sexually involved even though you know it would harm the other person, physically or emotionally?
- Uses his or her position, power, or influence to seduce others?
- Seeks out crowded places or events to look for vulnerable people?
- Tries to totally control your sexual expressiveness?
- Totally disregards any responsibility for the consequences of his or her sexual behavior?
- Thinks that what he or she does sexually is nobody's business?

R_x for Better Relationships

If you are in a relationship with a predator, it is time to move on, even if you enjoy the sex. There is no guarantee that therapy or counseling will keep a predator from returning to established patterns that can be dangerous.

Ask yourself, "How else can I make myself feel this good?" If you have no other way to express sexual pleasure than to be with a predator, your sexual repertoire is too narrow and too dependent on taking extreme risks with your own life.

Let go of connections to partners who have controlled you in the past. They still expect you to be a victim and will never let you be anything else. Remember, the power imbalance in your relationship was enjoyed by both of you. If you want to change and they don't, then you need to let go of them. Otherwise, they will find other willing partners and you will continue to experience problems in developing mutually respectful intimate relationships.

Seek counseling for yourself. Are you out "catching" in places that expose you to predators? Have you been in relationships with predators before? Without greater self-awareness, you may attract other partners who want to control you. And there are plenty of predators in this world who will allow you to be their prey.

You deserve better.

9

Clueless about Grief and Stress

Secret #9: If you don't know that you're vulnerable, you'll be hurt again.

When you're feeling anxious, frightened, lonely, or insecure, it's not unusual to turn to someone for sex, comfort, and support. The problem is that people under stress rarely try to protect themselves and are more likely to hurt themselves and others. The result is sex that they later regret.

A sense of haunting guilt and shame begins to color their relationships. Some people spend years avoiding partners and behaviors that they fear might expose them to similar pain. In these instances, one partner's vulnerability always leaves the other clueless.

If you expect that your partners will read your mind, see what makes you feel vulnerable, and be considerate of your feelings, you are being unrealistic and expecting way too much. On the other hand, if you cultivate relationships with people who know how to listen, you may be able to allow yourself to be vulnerable. You can tell friends or lovers what you need from them in order to feel supported and nurtured, and return the favor by asking them what they need from you.

If you can learn to express your feelings and listen to the feelings of your partner, you can begin to create a balance in your relationships and begin to feel less vulnerable. But the first step is to recognize that you are vulnerable. This chapter offers strategies for confronting and rebounding from the kind of experiences that frequently result in sex under stress, including:

1. Losing a long-term partner
2. An unintended pregnancy
3. Being incarcerated
4. Physical abuse

You or your partner may have had one or more of these experiences. But even if you haven't, these are all-too-human situations. Everyone is vulnerable in some way. Let's take a closer look at what links these circumstances to other stressful events, "the 9-11 syndrome."

Sex under Stress: Understanding the 9/11 Syndrome

Sex under stress frequently starts with a crisis for one or both partners. The pattern of using sex to feel better in a crisis was well documented before September 11, 2001. But after that day, when millions of people watched thousands of others die in New York City, Pennsylvania, and Washington, D.C., over and over again in terrifying replays on television, this pattern found its name.

You probably remember that day yourself. Traumatized

about the future, feeling vulnerable and insecure, it seemed as if the whole world heard the roar and felt the impact of the planes that destroyed the World Trade Center or part of the Pentagon or crashed to the ground. And you were not alone if you sought comfort, tenderness, and support in sex.

Stressful situations like war, natural disasters, earthquakes, floods, hurricanes, and tragic events at work or at home always have the effect of increasing human desire for closeness as a means to soothe feelings of despair. In a study of the effects of the 1992 earthquake in Los Angeles County on 900 women, we found that most reported that they had sex, some physical contact, or attempted to find someone whom they could be close to immediately following that event. Nine to ten months later, hospitals in Los Angeles confirmed significant increases in the number of babies delivered.

How Stress and Comfort Sex Works

Since stress works on our brains like a drug, any trauma can drag you into a "9/11" state of mind. Such was the case on an ordinary day at the office for Ricardo, a twenty-nine-year-old, New York–born Puerto Rican, and Abigail, a thirty-five-year-old administrative analyst.

Strangers riding an elevator, they were startled when suddenly the lights went out and the elevator lunged, then stopped dead. Ricardo told us the following story. When all their screams failed to hasten help, he and Abigail tried to make an escape plan. For the next two hours, they talked. They could hear repairmen a long distance off.

Abigail began to cry. It was lonely and cold, so Ricardo offered to sit closer. He wrapped his arms around her and they huddled together in a corner. They started to tell each other their life stories, jokes, recipes, anything to distract themselves from what was happening. Finally, both began to relax. At least they had each other.

Exhausted, Ricardo made a pallet with his coat. They lay together in the dark, warming, comforting, and singing to each other. One thing led to another and they had sex. Neither resisted; they just let their feelings take over. Several hours later, the door opened and they awkwardly stepped out.

"No regrets?" Ricardo asked.

"No regrets," Abigail replied.

They had experienced the 9/11 syndrome, but without any hurtful consequences. They were both rare and fortunate in this regard. The 9/11 syndrome is not new. People are likely to engage in comfort sex before, during, and after war or at any time in their lives when they are uncertain about the future. They may think that they will not have to face the consequences of their behavior.

Remember This Clue

Immediately after a crisis everyone needs to relieve stress. The following ways will have fewer unintended consequences than sex will, and more people will appreciate them:

- Call your family and friends. Check with them on a regular basis. Let them know how important they are to you. In catastrophic situations, we are all reminded how fragile and vulnerable we are.

- Seek out support groups to discuss your feelings. You will be helping others who need support, too.

- Strengthen your religious faith. Find opportunities to deepen your spiritual beliefs.

Losing a Long-Term Partner

What happens when your 9/11 stress involves the loss of someone you love? The threat of losing someone you know is scary enough, but when death takes away a loved one, your emotions peak and you discover that your capacity for making sexual decisions in your best interest breaks down. Loretta is an example.

Loretta's husband, David, a fifty-year-old, lifelong smoker, was dying of lung cancer and Loretta gathered him in her arms. She wanted him to feel her love once more. When his chest stopped moving, she held him tightly and cried on his shoulder, as she had done so many times before. Except now, he was gone. Her brother had to loosen her grasp on David's body. She was lost.

"I want to die, too," Loretta sobbed. "Please God, take me, too."

After the funeral, life returned to a regular pace, but Loretta still needed help. She knew it. So did Reverend Steve. He did not stop coming to visit her, and Loretta was grateful. They prayed together, took walks, and talked about everything, even David. Loretta felt safe and comfortable discussing her innermost feelings with Steve because he had known David before she had, and he was a minister. Steve, on the other hand, was attracted to Loretta, but was unwilling to stop visiting because she was so lonely. He was lonely, too.

Each time they parted, they would give each other a full-body hug, and one day, they just didn't stop there. Sex was so natural and full of passion for both—something they obviously wanted and needed. Loretta was surprised at her behavior. She had felt dead when David died, but Steve had helped her to feel something again. However, when he approached her for sex on the next visit, she had regrets.

"What are we doing? What would David think of me now? I had never planned to have sex again!"

Steve tried to console her, but felt it best to leave. He sent another minister to visit with her and avoided her at church when their eyes met.

What happened to Loretta and Steve is a familiar scenario. Neither was prepared for the sexual arousal that sprang from grief, their need to feel something other than sadness, and the 9/11 syndrome.

Sexual arousal between friends is common after the death of a loved one. If you have this experience, the problem is, like Loretta and Steve, you end up losing your loved one and your friend, too. The loss of two significant people in your life can be even harder to bear.

From the beginning of a crisis of loss, friends need to try extremely hard to pace their emotions. If you ever find yourself in this situation, and it is indeed common, here's what you will need to remember in order to keep your balance:

- Talk about your physical, emotional, and sexual needs instead of acting on them.
- Recognize that being emotionally close to each other can lead to sex.
- Realize that once you begin having sex, it is difficult to return to a nonsexual relationship.
- Accept that when a person's friendship is really treasured, it is best to avoid sexual contact or situations where the lines between friends and lovers are blurred or lost.

Remember, too, that as you get older, the loss of a committed partner, companion, and sex partner means you may soon be overwhelmed with offers from potential partners. Widows and widowers who seem to have little resistance to sex are particularly vulnerable to making bad sexual decisions.

The Stress of an Unintended Pregnancy

An unintended pregnancy can affect your relationships forever. It happened to Sylvia.

Growing up, Sylvia never felt very good about herself. She was always trying to please her alcoholic father to avoid the nightly whippings that she and her sisters received. When they weren't being beaten, their mother was, so Sylvia spent as much time away from home as she could.

Lonely and with no friends, Sylvia often walked around the schoolyard alone until she met Doris, who was just as poor, but did not seem to care. She smoked, drank, and introduced Sylvia to drugs. They would get high and laugh about their problems. Sylvia and Doris were tight. They started dressing, talking, and walking like each other. They felt more important that way, like they belonged.

Both of them started having sex with boys at about the same time, but it was Sylvia who first got pregnant. She was afraid to tell her parents until she began to "show." When her father found out, he made her leave home.

At age sixteen, Sylvia gave birth to twin girls and their father disappeared. She had yet to finish high school and faced raising her daughters alone, without parental support or involvement. In future sexual relationships, she not only would have to find someone who would accept and father her daughters, she needed someone who would, at times, father her.

The Stress of Being Incarcerated

Being jailed or detained, regardless of the length of time, can be a very traumatizing experience. It can invoke fear about being harmed physically, sexually, and emotionally. Regardless

R$_X$ for Healing from Unwanted Sexual Outcomes

We are all vulnerable to some extent because we are human. The hardest thing to do is to create a nurturing environment for ourselves so we can thrive. No one can do that for you, but others can help if you reach out and let them. It is never too late to try to rebuild your life. Here are some strategies to help:

- **Become sexually abstinent.** Sometimes years of abstinence are necessary to prepare yourself to be whole in a healthy relationship. Abstinence is the best thing you can do for yourself to let yourself develop intellectually and emotionally into a more mature individual who can make personal decisions in your own best interest.

- **Visit a health service or doctor.** Learn about STD/HIV protection, contraception, the morning-after pill, and HIV postexposure medications, just in case sex is forced on you.

- **Find new friends.** Look for others who are interested in the same short- and long-term personal goals for emotional support and setting goals you can attain.

- **Sign up for classes or a support group.** At church, in school, or in neighborhood organizations, seek out women or men as role models or mentors. Be selective. Choose people who continued their education and learned to put sex in its place.

- **Have nonsexual dates.** It takes practice to learn how to develop the common interests, trust, and communication skills that are necessary in nonsexual relationships. Don't worry if it feels strange at first not to have sex with someone you're dating.

> • **If you become sexually active again, take your time.** Think about what you want for yourself and your goals in life. Having one child before you were ready doesn't mean you have to have another one. Protect yourself from pregnancy until you are in control of what will happen if a baby is born.

of laws that prohibit sexual and physical violence in prison, it is a reality that detainees struggle to deal with every day. Johnson P. O'Brien was one of those people.

This redheaded Irish-Catholic from the south side of Chicago was once one of the most successful and most wanted burglars in the nation. He didn't like people and people didn't like him. When he was finally caught, he got six to ten years in prison.

His cellmate told Johnson to expect anal sex voluntarily or by force. Anal sex is the most painful and risky sexual practice because the lining of the rectum is extremely thin and easily torn. Blood vessels can be broken and cause you to bleed. Bacteria can enter the body and result in infections. At first Johnson fought back, but his cellmate was too big and too strong and repeated beatings just wore him down. He fell into the routine of being the "woman," or the "bottom," and waited for his parole. For the first time in his life, he could do little to avoid people, and in time, he became friends with his roommate.

While in prison, he would ask old girlfriends to visit him and pay guards with sexual favors if they would let him have sex with women in the prison's waiting room. When he was released Johnson never discussed these experiences with anyone. However, at the height of his sexual arousal, he would force his girlfriends to have anal sex, only this time he was the top and the woman was on the bottom. Now he was in control, or thought that he was.

Instead of obtaining help and support for what happened to him sexually, he reacted by forcing other sexual partners into the same position that once made him feel ashamed, humiliated, and powerless. When his attempts to dominate others failed to resolve his feelings or help him to rediscover his self-esteem, he developed unhealthy and aggressive sexual behavior.

When we meet people like Johnson, it's plain that they want to enjoy feelings of self-esteem and self-worth again. By learning new job skills, taking up hobbies, or going back to school for a high school equivalency or college degree, they can begin to get their bearings in society. But when it comes to sex, they frequently have to relearn everything they once knew before they were removed from society.

Sex should never diminish your self-esteem or that of your partner. It's bad enough that it makes you feel vulnerable, and even worse if it subjects others to the same pain. Guilt and shame have no place in a healthy sex life or sexual relationship. If partners are not willing to compromise or accept each other's need to heal, they need to at least help each other to let go and move on.

Being Physically or Verbally Abused

Pauline, a twenty-one-year-old from Galveston, Texas, was born unable to hear or speak. She was an excellent student and was determined to function in the world in spite of her health challenges, but dating was especially difficult until she met Renee. She was delighted to see that he could sign. More importantly, someone was finally paying attention to her.

But as their relationship deepened, Renee's behavior began to alarm Pauline. On a few occasions, she found him fol-

R$_X$ for Healing from New but Negative Sexual Patterns

Sex counseling is the key for you to:

- **Learn to discuss positive and negative feelings.** It is amazing how many men and women are aware only of their anger and rage. They never experience any positive feelings of joy. Keeping a daily record of things that happen and your personal feelings about them will help you notice a wider range of feelings.

- **Join weekly support groups that encourage non-violent emotional expression.** People with histories of incarceration often have difficulties in expressing emotions and resolving conflict, other than through physical aggression and violence. They need anger management or violence-reduction training. Patterns of communication that favor arguing or fighting are difficult to overcome without professional help.

- **Relearn former sexual patterns and discard recently learned behaviors.** New sexual patterns can be exciting, but they can make you feel guilty, ashamed, and depressed. It's also possible that sexual habits may have changed after years of experiencing pleasure from different sexual behaviors. In this case, it's important to discuss what you'd like to try sexually with your partner before getting into the habit of unexpectedly forcing him or her to do something unwillingly in the heat of the moment.

- **Stop having sex at all for a while.** Relearning requires that you have no sex until you select sexual behaviors that are satisfying but don't leave you feeling guilty and ashamed.

lowing her to work. When she confronted him, he hit her, only to break into tears. With passionate sex, he confessed his love and tried to make amends.

The pattern of Renee's abuse worsened, always with sex to smooth it over. After arguing, they shared some of their most intimate times. Pauline was as frightened by his anger as she was overcome with Renee's love and tenderness. She tried to get along by doing what he asked. But the more submissive she became, the more she was battered.

She came to us for a physical exam. After learning about her history and seeing how trapped she felt, we arranged for intake workers from a shelter for battered women to pick her up.

In an undisclosed location where Renee could not find her, Pauline received counseling and help to move to another city. We admired her tremendous courage in being able to accept help to start her life over and leave behind the controlling relationship. But we knew she would need a lot more help to keep from falling into the same pattern of sex and abuse in her future relationships.

The Inside Story

A history of abuse makes you vulnerable to making mistakes in future relationships. If you have been hit, kicked, punched, or threatened with harm, you are vulnerable to seeking another person who will also abuse you physically. If you have been verbally demeaned and devalued, you are prone to seek out new partners who will do the same to you. If you have been abused you will probably seek partners who will make your decisions and control you.

People who have been battered either physically or psychologically are also less likely than other people to initiate discussions about their past sexual histories with new sexual partners, get tested for STDs and HIV, and discuss which contraceptives they should use.

With professional help from a trained therapist, survivors of abuse can break this cycle. Without help, they are most likely to repeat it over again. Unfortunately, they often return to the same partner.

People in therapy and support groups gain many practical benefits. For example, if you were to join such a group, you could learn how to reduce your vulnerability by learning how to:

- **Recognize your attraction to abusive partners.** Vulnerable people need to be taught how to develop relationships with partners who offer them respect and value rather than put-downs.

- **Practice self-defense and use it for self-protection.** Using self-defense can increase a survivor's risk of her partner becoming more abusive. And it may be better to leave than to fight. But each situation should be evaluated to decide on the best action to take and when to take it. Survivors need strategies that give them options in situations where they believe sex is the only solution.

- **Develop greater confidence and better communication skills.** Seeking the help of friends and professionals who can observe interactions or listen to arguments with a partner gives survivors opportunities to receive coaching in skills they lack. Sometimes, others who love and respect you can see your relationship problems before you can.

Being a survivor and not a victim is a daily responsibility that takes work, like a job. It requires new skills and abundant practice to learn how to select friends who will not take advantage of you. If you have experienced trauma in the recent or distant

155

past, if you have ever been controlled and manipulated or emotionally wounded by a partner, you have every reason to be very careful about the future relationships that you develop. You also have every reason to be very selective about future sexual partners. Take the time needed to get to know people who are close to you, not out of fear but out of the expectation that people have to earn your trust, your friendship, and your comfort in order for you to be vulnerable in their presence.

Sometimes letting go of relationships that make you feel sexually vulnerable is the only way to find your strength again.

10

Clueless Obsessions and Commitments

Secret #10: Sex should be a choice, not a compulsion.

No one wants to admit that he or she is willing to be led around like a trained animal waiting for the next command. But having a mental illness or sexual obsession is like that. Sadly, it seems that a lot of people become sexual casualties of illnesses like manic-depression or give in to hypersexuality instead of getting professional help to maintain normal sex lives.

Today, many people in supportive families and sexual relationships live with a mental illness and its symptoms without major disruptions as long as they continue their medication and psychotherapy with a trained professional. On the other hand, without family support and resources, a mental disorder can be a major disruption. So when someone seems to be out of control, loved ones need to let them know that they need to be evaluated. Their partners cannot stand by, remain silent, and allow self-destructive behavior to continue and then claim to be clueless about a drug overdose, incarceration, suicide, rape, or alcoholic binges.

Such was the case for the patients whose stories you are about to read.

Reginald's Story: A Script for Obsession

Reginald was like a fish out of water on her side of town, but he was picking up Tonya for dinner. When he saw her, he got an erection and began to visualize what she would do for him later that night.

"Hi, Baby, you're late."

"Sorry, Tonya, I got lost," Reginald apologized. He did not want to upset her, so he leaned over and put his finely chiseled lips on her full mouth and gave her a big kiss.

Reginald's friends told him he was "pussy whipped." But he didn't care. He would have driven to hell to pick up Tonya if she had asked.

Reginald had little sexual experience other than with his first wife when he asked Tonya out on a dare from his buddies at a bar. To his amazement, she was in college. She was intelligent and she had dreams of her own, but was more streetwise than her boarding school–bred lover. She knew that if she could control this little "preppy" in bed, he could help her pay some of her bills.

Reginald was too happy to pay. He made all sorts of excuses to his boss, friends, and ex-wife to obtain money to make Tonya happy. At nightclubs after work, he was barely conscious of anything but thinking about what he would do to get her in bed again.

Tonya would tease him with her seasoned bag of tricks and make him beg for sex. She would torture him by parading around in short, lacy outfits that showed her breasts and smooth, toned torso. His jaw dropped the first time she tore off her panties and kept her knee-high boots on during sex.

He was in heaven. The thought that he could be heading for disaster never entered his mind.

Dorothy's Story: Problems with Celibacy

In any long-term, mutually rewarding relationship, it would be impossible to even imagine the intensity of lusting for your partner every day, being totally worn out from sex every night, keeping a demanding job, raising kids, and trying to have a balanced life. Few would want to try—for long.

Ironically, celibacy can be just as challenging. By definition, it is not a sexual obsession. Celibacy is a commitment, a vow to follow rules that don't allow sex under any circumstances. As such, it is different and more extreme than being abstinent.

When people are sexually abstinent, they are temporarily not having sex for any of a variety of reasons. Usually they have no partner, are taking a break from sex, have an illness, lack sexual desire, or have a disability. Given their choice and the right opportunity, they would probably prefer to be sexually active.

Being celibate also differs from being sexually inactive in its power to narrow a person's options to a point that leads at best to confusion and at worse to a kind of self-punishing compulsion. Dorothy's story is an example of this dilemma.

Growing up, Dorothy was devoted to her best friend, Susan, to the exclusion of all other competing interests. They shared the same values and religion and each girl felt that they were meant to be together forever. They went to the same

R$_x$ for Healing

When you are "pussy whipped" like Reginald, there's no boundary between lust and love. So many feelings can confuse you. Even if you are sexually experienced, it is romantic and exciting to discover the infinite pleasure you can experience with good sex. You begin to think that you will never feel that much love for anyone else— or ever feel that good having sex again.

That kind of euphoric response is as typical of a sexual compulsion or an obsession as anxiety or depression. But once you acknowledge it, you need to get a grip. Here's what we would recommend to help you move toward getting out of the danger zone:

- **Ask yourself, "Does my lover share and fit into my short- and long-term personal and profes-sional goals?"** We once knew a professional man who was being "whipped." In spite of advice from family and friends, he got married. The relationship lasted seven years before he realized that he and his lover had absolutely nothing in common except sex and their daughter. However, that proved not enough to sustain a marriage or committed relationship.

- **Abstain from sex if you ever feel you cannot live without it.** Being abstinent for a month or two really helps to highlight the strength of your non-sexual relationship and what you have in common. If your relationship was meant to be, those qualities will keep you together long after one or both of you is no longer able to perform sexually as you might have in the past.

- **Make a concerted effort to be seen with your lover at public and family events.** Reginald needed to invite his partner to parties with his friends and parents. If Tonya did not fit in, that may have told him something—either his friends and family were snobbish or Tonya wasn't the kind of partner he would feel comfortable with in other places.

- **Don't have sex without protection, no matter what your partner allows.** Reginald needed to ask himself, "If I'm not asking Tonya to be my life partner, what am I doing having unprotected sex with her?"

college and lived together quite happily, successfully suppressing their sexuality when other teenagers were exploring it. Then disaster struck. In their junior year, Susan was discovered to have a brain tumor and barely survived surgery. Stunned initially, Dorothy and Susan took vows to remain true to each other no matter what happened next, and Dorothy pledged her lifelong celibacy, as well. For her part, Susan was no longer interested in sex or motivated to really try to live at all.

Courageously, Dorothy took over all their household chores. She balanced their budget to adjust for Susan's loss of income. She hired a nurse to care for Susan while she was working. She did the laundry, cooked, and cleaned, leaving little time for herself. Each day she looked for signs of Susan's recovery even though the doctors had not been optimistic.

Dorothy tried to adjust as best as she could. But as years passed, a yearning for physical contact emerged and became stronger and stronger. She began to wonder if she could ever feel sexual pleasure with anyone. Now in her early thirties, she could not ignore the way men and other women looked at her. She knew they found her attractive.

Eddie was one of the ones always staring at her. He was handsome and married. She remembered his wife never came to the office parties, but office gossip was that they didn't seem to be spending much time with each other. During the holiday office party she and Eddie talked and she discovered he was unhappy in his marriage. They consoled one another and danced until she noticed Eddie, who had pulled her close, had an erection. Having no experience to fall back on, she couldn't decide what she should do. Encouraged by her passive response, Eddie kissed her. Only then did she pull away and say, "Don't do that again."

He apologized contritely. Dorothy left and went home.

That evening she took a bath, hoping to rid herself of her mounting sexual tension. She thought of Eddie. Her religion discouraged self-touching, but she felt she had to do something even if it took rationalizing later. She positioned herself in the tub so warm water from the faucet ran over her labia and clitoris. Soon, she became orgasmic. But she felt so guilty it was hardly worth it. She had no idea that she could be celibate on the outside while lusting on the inside.

The Inside Story

In reality, Dorothy was no longer celibate but sexually abstinent. She was torn between honoring her relationship vows and her genuine sexual feelings. Her choice to be celibate was admirable, but in her changed circumstances, it was hard to maintain. Learning to ignore sexual feelings doesn't allow you to develop a sexual pattern or know what sexual pattern that you might be compatible with. The depth of your sexual feelings is unknown. Moreover, it takes adult social skills to develop friendships with common interests, shared values, and trust after childhood.

Celibate people are often caught off guard and rush to have sex when they are attracted to someone who finally pays attention to them sexually. They may not know about the latest forms of sexual exploitation, STDs, drugs to enhance sex, Internet dating, blind dates, sex parties, and what to avoid.

Dorothy's method of suppressing her sexual needs was no longer working. She needed much more information and the permission to act on it. Fortunately, there were a number of options available to her. First, she could include Susan in her dilemma. Foolishly, but selflessly, Dorothy actually believed it improper to burden Susan with her sexual needs and didn't give her life partner a chance to discuss a solution acceptable to both of them. Both sincerely needed the other's permission to explore their changing sexual needs and desires.

Dorothy also needed to tap into resources available in her community to help her with caretaking. Dorothy had unnecessarily limited her social support. She desperately needed much more help to free up time so she could have regularly scheduled outings and vacations.

There were also physical consequences to celibacy. Dorothy needed to prepare herself physically as well as emotionally to have sexual intercourse for the first time if she expected to enjoy it.

Samantha's Story: The Challenge of Mental Illness

At best, symptoms of intense sexual desire are confusing to the person experiencing them. This confusion is compounded by the difficult challenge of mental illness. Even professionals can

Remember This Clue

The best lovers are friends first: A friend is someone with whom you can share your feelings, without fear of being hurt.

Rx for Better Sex

Not having sexual intercourse for a long time results in some shrinkage of the vagina, and self-lubrication may take longer. This can cause pain with intercourse that must be controlled with a lubricant and relaxation techniques. When the penis or dildo is entering the vagina, push down on your bottom, as hard as you can, and push out the muscle you learned to tighten with Kegel exercises. The vagina will open and penetration will be less traumatic.

be confused. We have seen compulsive sexual behavior misdiagnosed by doctors who do not understand that in some cases, the reason for the hypersexuality is a mental illness, like a bipolar disorder.

Patients who are bipolar or manic-depressive have mood swings, or exaggerated spurts of being highly active (manic) and extremely productive, followed by crashing (depression), a period of nonproductivity and feelings of hopelessness. Feelings of hypersexuality accompany the manic phases of the mood cycle, and individuals with bipolar disorder may have high rates of sexual activity.

In men, the compulsive need for sex is often considered tantamount to being a good lover. When men use drugs like methamphetamines or yohimbine to further heighten their sexual desire and performance, their compulsion can go on without anybody commenting. In women, however, hypersexual behavior is more likely to be called "nymphomania." Society is usually eager to unmask this condition in women, labeling them freaks or whores. Samantha, known as the Harvard "ho" when we met her, fit those labels.

It certainly wasn't apparent to Samantha, a high school

valedictorian on a full academic scholarship to Harvard, that she had a problem. However, her roommate complained about the days she spent in bed followed by the days she spent partying all day, writing papers, and pumping out homework assignments for which she always received "A's." She considered herself a high-maintenance genius, but her college friends thought that she was over the top. When her family visited campus, Samantha would take them on a whirlwind tour and whisk them away. It wasn't until her best friend called her parents because Samantha had not returned to the dorm from a party that they finally launched into rescue mode. In the past, they were so proud of her good grades that they overlooked her wild behavior and thought that she was just letting off steam.

When they canvassed crack crash pads, they found her unconscious and whisked her to the hospital to pump her stomach. Samantha was full of enough drugs to kill her. Finally cleared to leave the hospital, Samantha was brought by her frightened parents to see a team of mental health professionals who diagnosed her bipolar disorder.

We discussed her symptoms so that she could easily identify when to change her behavior. The one symptom that she simply could not seem to change with or without her own recreational drug use was an insatiable need for sex.

Positive Action Steps

When you hear a girlfriend saying "I can have sex with ten guys and still want more," take notice. That's not sexual desire, that's part of her illness. If you care about her, make sure that she is being treated and is on her medicine, every day.

Samantha's academic productivity continued and she learned how to understand how being manic and depressed affected her sexuality.

And what about you? When you begin to feel "horny" and start thinking about sexual contact a lot, don't wait to see what happens next. Take positive action. For example, you can:

- Increase your physical activity every day by walking more, at a minimum twenty or thirty minutes through-out the day.
- Go to the gym or play a sport.
- Learn yoga or meditation for relaxation.
- Channel your sexual energy into constructive activities, projects that do not increase your risks for being taken advantage of sexually or you taking advantage of anyone else.

If these feelings persist, it wouldn't hurt to get professional help. A professional will teach you how to:

- Select partners who will not take advantage of you.
- Tell partners about your illness.
- Cope with possible rejection from partners without returning to unhealthy behaviors and destructive drug use to numb your pain.

11

Clueless No More

On the afternoon of her appointment, Señora Sanchez, a seventy-year-old widow with long black hair and green eyes, was nervous. Her face flushed as she started telling us her story, but after a while, the words flowed easily.

She said that the only sex that she had ever had was with her husband, and the only sex she knew was what he told her they would have. They met during their senior year of high school and married after graduation. He was the champion of the quickie until he died fifty-four years later.

Now, she said, she had met a man who was interested in her, and she wasn't sure what to do. He had been a patient at the local hospital where she volunteered. Señor Rojas was a dapper, charming gentleman, even in his hospital gown. When he laid eyes on the señora, he said, she took his pain away. Señor Rojas had a great sense of humor. Every day until he was discharged, they spent hours telling each other stories about their lives, their children, and what it was like growing older.

Señor Rojas risked being turned down and asked the señora to lunch. She accepted, and they dated for weeks. It was at that point that Señora Sanchez sought our help to think about what she should do. It was a wise decision. After a few counseling sessions, she felt encouraged and better prepared to take a chance on having a sexual relationship again. And we gave her a few ideas to help Mr. Rojas succeed, although he seemed to be doing quite well on his own.

On a day that she knew she was ready for sex, she allowed Señor Rojas to take her to his home, play her favorite music, spray his house with her favorite fragrance, serve her favorite foods, and make love to her on satin sheets. He proposed marriage not long after.

The day before the wedding, Señora Sanchez visited the grave of her first husband.

"My darling Diego, you were my first love and I miss the life we had together—except the way that you loved me." She sighed, holding a single rose. "I hope that you approve of my second husband and rejoice in knowing that I am happy. For the first time in my life, I have learned to enjoy the pleasures of lovemaking. I pray that you understand that sex is an important part of my life. I wish that I could have shared what I am feeling with you, but since I cannot, I am grateful that God gave me one more chance to experience this kind of love before my life is over."

Leaving the rose behind, she walked back to her car.

The Inside Story—The Importance of Knowing Yourself

You've probably given a lot of thought to your own sexual history as you've been reading this book. That's exactly what we hoped would happen. Self-knowledge is crucial to happiness.

By now, it's no secret to you that how much you know about yourself makes the difference between having a relationship that works and having one that doesn't.

With her first husband, Señora Sanchez had limited self-knowledge. She never asserted her personal feelings. She kept her hopes and dreams to herself. With Señor Rojas, she overcame her insecurities. She reached out for help to achieve real fulfillment. She felt more willing to express love and be loved than she had felt before. Why? Señor Rojas brought out her best qualities. He encouraged her feelings of self-esteem.

Several things activate self-esteem:

- A realistic sense of your strengths and weaknesses
- The ability to recuperate from the results of past sexual decisions
- The willingness to take your time before making new sexual decisions
- The ability to refuse to let others define you
- The ability to resist letting age, illness, or loss of a loved one permanently reduce your sense of worth

Señora Sanchez also wisely took her time before adding sex to her budding relationship. She got to know her potential partner. They became best friends before they became lovers.

What about you?

You may not be ready for some potential partners, but you may have outgrown others. You may be ready for some kinds of sex, and you may never be ready to try other kinds.

The following assignments will help you understand yourself and relate to your partner better. If he is the right partner for you, the insights gained from these assignments will validate your choice to remain together and enhance your sexual relationship. If he's not right for you, use these insights to change your life now and reach for happiness in a different emotional and sexual relationship.

Assignment One: Take an Inventory

1. On a sheet of paper, make three long columns.

2. Label the far-left column "My Partners." List the name of every sexual partner you remember. Number them. Be honest. Name every one. Add more sheets of paper if you need to.

3. Label the middle column "Acceptable Acts." List the things that you did with each partner that you enjoy remembering, whether the behavior was sexual (e.g., a particular position) or emotional (e.g., a decision to break up with a partner who was already married). Don't get caught up with memories of who was the cutest, where you dated, or who had the best clothes or hottest body. Concentrate on actions.

4. Label the last column "Unacceptable Acts." List the sexual things that you did with each partner that you do not like remembering. Even if you remember some good times, even if you cared about a particular partner, if any act made you feel vulnerable, afraid, or ashamed, it was unacceptable. List it.

5. Put your inventory aside for a few hours. Then return to it.

6. Take another sheet of paper and divide it into three columns.

7. Label the far-left column "My Strengths." List all of the positive qualities that your sexual experiences and partners have brought out in you.

8. Label the middle column "My Weaknesses." List the negative or vulnerable qualities that your sexual experiences and partners brought out in you.

MY HISTORY

My Partners	Acceptable Acts	Unacceptable Acts

MY QUALITIES

My Strengths	My Weaknesses	My Results

9. Label the last column "My Results." List where your various relationships have led you. What have been the outcomes of the decisions and choices you made?

Assignment Two: Look for Patterns

Look closely at both charts now.

1. If a partner made you feel vulnerable, depressed, insecure, afraid, embarrassed, or humiliated, cross that person's name off the list. The more vulnerable you are made to feel in a relationship, the worse the qualities it brings out in you and the more negatively you will be affected. *If you are currently in a relationship with someone whose name you crossed off, recognize that that relationship is already at a dead end and it is probably not in your best interest to try to revive it, no matter how much time you've invested in it.*

2. Look again at the list labeled "Unacceptable Acts." Cross each act off the list. As you do, recognize that each item must be eliminated from your life, too. You do not need to repeat the behavior that it represents in your future sex life if you choose to let it go. It's up to you to change it, let it go, or get professional help to do so and be more selective about what you want to do in the future. No relationship is perfect, but every happy relationship has a boundary between acceptable and unacceptable acts. Divide experiences that make you ashamed of yourself from those you still feel good about when the afterglow has dimmed. *If you are currently in a relationship without such a boundary or bottom line, recognize that you both need to talk about this now. You may not be able to save the relationship, but if you can talk and listen, you have a chance.*

3. Circle the name of each partner who made you feel open

and willing to love and be loved, feelings that brought out the best in you. There are bound to be rough times in any relationship, especially those that have stood the test of time. People don't get it right every day, but people who try to understand each other's moods and wishes have a better chance than most. *If you are currently in a relationship that's in your best interest, continue to protect each other's vulnerabilities and try the techniques and the prescriptions we've recommended for communication and greater self-awareness to enhance your time together.*

The Wyatts' Rules

Over the past three decades, we've counseled countless people about how to build stronger, more emotionally satisfying relationships based on their particular history. If the time has come for you to enjoy a more dynamic relationship, we want to stress ten rules:

Rule 1: Stop being one of the walking wounded.

If someone has done you wrong sexually in the past, don't fall into the trap of expecting sympathy for the rest of your life. Ultimately, it is up to you to get the help you need to leave the past behind. Reflect on the effect that sex has had on your life, heal, learn from the bad experiences, and move on. Reading this book was a courageous start. It means that you are going after the happiness you really want and are not afraid to face your fears.

If you've been hurt, the best thing to do is forgive yourself as well as the person involved. Don't waste precious time and energy trying to hold on to your anger or shame. You don't have to forget what happened—and you certainly should protect yourself from being hurt again. But each day provides opportunities for you to start over in defining your sex life. Procrastination won't move you, and anger won't heal you, but forgiveness can do both.

If you can't get beyond your pain, then take this as a sign to seek help. We recommend you stop having sex until your therapist gives you a green light. Keep all relationships casual until you are sure you can relate to someone else with mutual respect, honesty, and healthy behavior. Avoid taking your past problems out on everyone in your future.

Rule 2: Get to know yourself better.

Take some time for yourself for a change. Retreat. Go to a relaxing and private place where you can be alone yet feel safe. Maximize your solitude and minimize distractions. Try to eat very light food and drink plenty of water as a way of cleansing your body. Meditate to clear your mind and spirit of painful memories. Then think about your boundaries and your desires and make better choices.

If you're like most people, you already know what you need sexually. Use your head, and your heart will follow.

Rule 3: Clear out bad influences.

Stop hanging around people who have no consideration for your feelings and interfere with your right to be you. You know who they are. They don't respect you. They are jealous of you. They try to put you down or rarely have anything good to say about you. They may encourage you to break up with someone and then turn around and try to date that same person. They encourage you to do certain things and then talk about you when you do. They don't create a sense of well-being in you and can lower your self-esteem.

In a relationship, it is important to avoid people who you know are making the same mistakes you're trying to fix. Pity parties are only for people who are pitiful.

Don't follow the crowd unless it's going where you want to go. Disconnect, even though it's not going to be easy. Sometimes it will be money, a career, or a higher social status that compels you to seek the advice or company of people who encourage you to get involved with dangerous sexual behavior. Or you may go along despite your better judgment because you crave excitement and feel lonely or bored with your life. Whenever you are tempted, remember what sexual behaviors you crossed off your list and out of your life.

Rule 4: Surround yourself with people who support your values.

You will never regret making the effort to find friends with similar goals. This is especially important if you are in a relationship that you want to work. You and your partner need friends who are working on their relationships and supporting yours.

The values that you should be practicing include:

- **Trust.** Do you mean what you say and say what you mean and never mean saying it? You could spend the rest of your life working on this goal. But few things could be more worthwhile than making the effort in your relationships. Being confident that you can count on someone to follow through in good times and bad times relieves unnecessary stress and allows each of you to try to solve problems without being afraid of losing the other person.
- **Spirituality.** No matter what your religion is, your relationship with God matters. It can help you to develop boundaries around how you want to express your sexuality. Do you have spiritual beliefs? Don't hide them. Let them guide you toward more loving, caring behavior in all your relationships.
- **Tradition.** Your ancestors passed along guidelines for

respect and family life through your parents and others. Do you have a sense of family tradition? Accept it. Enhance it. Grow with it. Keep the best parts of the tradition alive and get rid of the parts that limit your potential to love and respect others.

- **Responsibility.** Do you expect certain things from others because of their gender, or because of yours? Being clear about what you expect and what you think is expected of you based on your gender role helps to clarify your sexuality. Talk about gender roles with your partner. Do you have the same expectations? Push for clarity. Expect to enhance your excitement by accepting responsibility for your gender role *and* expand it. Practice responsibility with your friends.

- **Honesty.** Do you tell the truth about yourself and your sexuality, no matter how painful the truth is? People who find happiness in relationships know and accept their sexuality. So don't hide it, lie about it, or be ashamed of being sexual. Everyone is a sexual being. Use what you have! Sexual pleasure is a natural means of self-expression. As we've said throughout this book, no one—not your teachers, parents, ministers, favorite celebrities, or congressmen—can tell you what feels good to you. Your instincts will. Friends and partners who support your efforts to be yourself will affirm your instincts.

Your values may change with age and shifting priorities. But if your values are solid, no one should be able to violate or change them but you. Fight to preserve them for yourself if someone challenges your ideas.

Conversely, recognize that you cannot force a change in your partner's values. At best, you can only persuade. If your values are contradictory or incompatible, let the person go before you let your values go.

Rule 5: Expect your sex life to change.

This is a difficult rule for most people. It's hard to get used to expecting change. You may realize that something about your sex life needs to change, but if you are accustomed to an established pattern, you might be tempted to stay with it even if it isn't working for you. You may fear changing more than you fear the problems you complain about.

Making changes in your sex life can be difficult because you may have to give up some rewards. For example, you may be holding on to the belief that you should be married or in a committed relationship. But if a marriage or a relationship eludes you, you may need to create a different set of expectations for your sexual happiness.

Does this contradict the idea of fighting for your values? Not if you maintain honesty as a core value.

Rule 6: Practice active communication.

- Look into the eyes of the person talking.
- Repeat what they just said.
- Don't respond to what they said until you've confirmed that you heard what they meant.

These are the rules for active listening. But equally important is the art of what could be called active watching. In sexual communication, it's as important to pay attention to people's actions as it is to pay attention to what they say.

"What did my partner's behavior say? What does it mean?" Those are tough but inspired questions. A contradiction between words and behaviors either means that the behavior reflects true feelings, or your partner does not communicate in a straightforward way.

If your partner's behavior speaks to you, don't ignore your instincts. Listen.

Model the open communication that you want from your

partner. Let your words *and* your behavior express your feelings, expectations, needs, pain, and joy. Expect and encourage your partner to do the same. Keep the circuit open. Try to talk to each other intimately about your feelings for fifteen minutes each day. If this proves difficult or impossible, though, don't worry. "I love you" sounds great, but being treated in a loving way is better.

Rule 7: Control your own sexual boundaries.

Are there sexual behaviors that you will not engage in? What are they? Why do your boundaries exclude or include certain sexual practices?

It is important to know your answers to these questions because someone else is likely to ask you. You will have to defend your boundaries over and over again. Be prepared to respond with confidence.

Moreover, when you set a boundary, be prepared to give up friends, lovers, and sexual experiences. You can't have everything and have boundaries, too. Boundaries can protect you from people or experiences that are not in your best interests.

Given different circumstances, you may need to change your boundaries, but do so slowly. Sex is a wonderful experience and a great way to relate to yourself or to anyone else. But it has been distorted and overrated by people who exploit, control, and titillate others.

"Can I live without sex?" we are frequently asked.

Absolutely. If you are not in a relationship and choose not to be sexually active, the only thing you need to be concerned about is what are you are going to do with your sex drive. It is normal to be physically close to someone and to feel sexually gratified, though. Accept your need for sex. If you choose not to act on those feelings, then you'll have to find other outlets for them that are healthy for you. If you think that you can pray away or ignore your sex drive, you may place yourself in situations where you have sex suddenly, without preparation, with the wrong person, and under the wrong circumstances.

Rule 8: If something's wrong, focus on the problem, not the person.

Problems are inevitable in any relationship. However, if you love the person, sometimes it's hard to separate them from their problems. If you focus on a problem, though, it is easier to help your partner work toward solving it. Adopt a strategy of focusing on the problem.

Accusing, threatening, and blaming your partner for having problems that he or she won't solve can only distance the two of you. This will make it harder to communicate as well as harder to solve the problem.

Verbal insults like "You are a jerk!" or "You are a lousy lover!" hurt the person and do not address the problem. Rarely, if ever, do people improve their sexual performance or their relationships because they were insulted or belittled into doing so. If there is a problem, learn how to communicate about it in such a way that your partner can understand. Otherwise, you will be just talking to yourself. In the long run, remember that if your partner has a problem, so do you if you want to stay in the relationship.

Rule 9: Stay in the moment.

Don't get caught up reliving the past or anticipating what will happen in the future. The future is composed of what you are doing now, so try to savor it. If you ever start to question your ability to face your realities, try to remember words that reaffirm and appreciate your strength.

And don't forget our affirmation:

My gift is everything that I am. I have the capacity for love, passion, and a belief in God. I have the strength and the intelligence to stand up for what I believe in. I will share my gift only with those who earn my love, honesty, trust, and respect. But I will *only* share. My gift belongs to God and me. I will not give my gift away.

Rule 10: Never give up believing you can have a dynamic sex life.

Mutually satisfying sex depends on two people believing that they deserve friendship, love, and respect—from each other. Remember Señora Sanchez? She understood this perfectly. She had a strong and positive sense of herself as a loving and caring person. Her story teaches us the power of cultivating self-love and mutual respect.

In sexual relationships that work, partners eventually develop and cherish a renewed sense of adventure. Trusting each other and sharing emotions, partners can enjoy sex in ways—safe, tender, and passionate—that are good for both of them because they both know exactly what they are doing. We truly hope that after reading this book, you are ready to make your next move closer to a sex life that works for both of you.

Resources

Looking for more information about sex and your health? Here's a list of resources that may help.

National Organizations

The American Association of Gynecologic Laparoscopists
13021 East Florence Avenue
Sante Fe Springs, CA 90670–4505
Telephone: (800) 554–AAGL [(800) 554–2245] or
   (562) 946–8774
Email: generalmail@aagl.com
www.aagl.com

American Association of Sex Educators, Counselors,
   and Therapists
P.O. Box 5488
Richmond, VA 23220-0488
Email: AASECT@aasect.org
www.aasect.org/Home

The American Board of Sexology
2431 Aloma Avenue, Suite 277
Winter Park, FL 32792
Telephone: (407) 635–1641
Email: billeast@cfl.rr.com
www.sexologist.org
The information on this Web site was pioneered by William Masters,
   Margaret Sanger, Michel Foucalt, and others and lists certified ther-
   apists within the United States and abroad.

American Foundation for Urologic Disease
1128 North Charles Street
Baltimore, MD 21201
Telephone: (800) 433–4215 or (410) 468–1800
Email: impotence@afud.org
www.impotence.org
This group's Web site discusses erectile dysfunction and treatment
   options. Chat rooms are available on this site.

American Psychological Association
750 First Street, NE
Washington, DC 20002–4242
Telephone: (800) 374–2721 or (202) 336–5500
www.apa.org/about/contact.html

Association of Black Psychologists
P.O. Box 55999
Washington, DC 20040–5999
Telephone: (202) 722–0808
Email: admin@abpsi.org
www.abpsi.org/contact.html

National Uterine Fibroids Foundation
P.O. Box 9688
Colorado Springs, CO 80932–0688
Phone: (719) 633–3454 or (877) 553–6833
www.nuff.org/about_leadership.htm

Planned Parenthood Federation of America, Inc.
434 West 33rd Street
New York, NY 10001
Telephone: (212) 541–7800
Fax: (212) 245–1845
www.plannedparenthood.org
Planned Parenthood's Web site lists resources within the United States
   and throughout the world.

Rainn (Rape, Abuse, Incest, National Network)
  National Sexual Assault Hotline
1–800–656–HOPE (4673)
Free and confidential, twenty-four hours a day, seven days a week.
www.rainn.org
This Web site allows users to find counselors in their community who
  can assist them.

www.ojp.usdoj.gov/ovc/help/isa.htm
This Web site provides international listings for those who have suf-
  fered from incest or sexual abuse and need to know where to go for
  help.

SIECUS (Sexuality Information and Education Council
  of the United States)
New York Office
130 West 42nd Street, Suite 350
New York, NY 10036–7802
Telephone: (212) 819–9770
Fax: (212) 819-9776
Email: siecus@siccus.org

Washington, D.C., Office
1706 R Street, NW
Washington, DC 20009
Telephone: (202) 265–2405
Fax: (202) 462–2340

Hotlines

National AIDS Hotline
Telephone: (800) 342–AIDS (2437)
www.ashastd.org/nah
This Web site provides the latest information in treatment options,
  provides a chat room, and has a hotline for Spanish speakers.

National STD/HIV Hotline
Telephone: (800) 227–8922
STD counselors are available twenty-four hours a day, seven days a
  week.

Support Groups

COSA (originally stood for Co-dependents of Sex Addicts)
Telephone: (763) 537–6904
www.cosa-recovery.org
An organization for those affected by a sex addict's behavior.

S-ANON (for family members and friends of sex addicts)
P.O. Box 111242
Nashville, TN 37222–1242
Telephone: (615) 833–3152
Email: sanon@sanon.org
www.sanon.org

Sex Addicts Anonymous
Telephone: (800) 477–8191
www.saa-recovery.org
Sex Addicts Anonymous is perhaps the largest and most established of
the recovery groups. Membership is diverse—straight, gay, married,
single—and the international organization is especially strong.

Sex Compulsives Anonymous
Telephone: (800) 977–HEAL (4325)
www.sca-recovery.org
This group's membership is some cities is largely gay. An individual
can locate the telephone number to call for information on meeting
locations in his or her area and can locate a sponsor who can help
put together a program to help him or her succeed in reaching sexual sobriety.

Sex and Love Addicts Anonymous
Telephone: (781) 255–8825
www.slaafws.org
This group offers assistance to those suffering with compulsive relationships and sex obsessions.

Sexaholics Anonymous
Telephone: (615) 331–6230
www.sa.org
SA defines sexual sobriety in the strictest terms—sex with a marital
partner only.

Web Sites and Links

Abstinence

www.abstinence.net/about
Advocates abstinence until marriage and provides resources within the United States and throughout the world.

Erectile Dysfunction

www.niddk.nih.gov/health/urolog/pubs/impotnce/impotnce.htm
Discusses a common sexual dysfunction in men.

www.sexhealth.org/problems/premature.shtml
Discusses premature ejaculation and introduces the "squeeze technique" and how to apply it.

Female Sexuality and Aging

www.menopause.org
Email: info@menopause.org
Gives women information about the effects of menopause on their sex lives and their health and provides referrals to reputable health care providers.

www.americanmenopause.org
Provides help for women with menopause issues.

www.menopause.org/otherwebresources/outsidena.html
Menopause resources outside of the United States.

Male Sexuality and Aging

seniorhealth.about.com/library/usercontent/uc040801a.htm
Describes the symptoms that characterize andropause in men as they get older, such as reduced sex drive and difficulty in achieving an erection, and so on.

Puberty

www.puberty101.com/p_pubgirls.shtml
Explains puberty stages for girls.

www.puberty101.com/p_pubguys. shtml
Explains puberty stages for boys.

Recreational Drugs

www.a1b2c3.com/drugs
Describes all known recreational drugs and their effects.

Responsible Sex

vanderbiltowc.wellsource.com/dh/content.asp?ID=671
Explains the importance of discussing sexual histories with partners
  before engaging in sexual intimacy.

www.mwsexual.com/readingroom/ articles/using-condoms.htm
Gives tips on how to use condoms and the importance of being sexually responsible.

Sex Addictions

www.cyberaa.com/Discussion/discussion.html
Provides a chat room where other cybersex addicts can find support
  during their recovery.

www.cybersexualaddiction.com
Information regarding 12-step programs for addressing cybersex
  addiction.

www.sexualrecovery.com/resources/articles/lovept2.php
Discusses sexual addiction and low self-esteem to helps the addict to
  seek resources for recovery.

Sexual Fitness

www.geocities.com/steve4502/vagex.html
Explains Kegel exercises to strengthen the vagina.

Sexual Pleasure

health.discovery.com/centers/sex/sexpedia/erogenous.html
Talks about areas other than the obvious sex organs that can provide
  sexual pleasure.

www.sexscape.org/sexscape.cgi?qnum=82&searchword=lubricants
Answers questions about lubricants.

Sex Therapy

www.mastersandjohnson.com
Deals with relational and sexual therapy and sexual compulsivity and
addiction, and trauma-based disorders.

content.health.msn.com/content
Allows users to pose questions about sexual issues to various medical
journalists who post answers to this site.

www.aasect.org/results.cfm?type=&State=California
Provides the names of sex therapists, educators, and counselors in
California who men can go to receive help with their sexual issues.
Lists local address, phone numbers, and doctors' Web sites and
credentials.

coolnurse.healthology.com/focus_index.asp
Features accredited therapists' video and audio presentations on a
wide range of sexual issues. Visitors can submit questions via
email.

www.drdrew.com/Office/ask.asp
The link to the Los Angeles–based "Dr. Drew Radio Show." Visitors
can submit questions on all major sex topics to Dr. Drew.

Sexual Social Protocol

www.canoe.ca/LifewiseHeartVal00/0316_fake.html
Discusses the fact that men can and do fake orgasms.

www.celebrateintimacy.com/lauralewis.html
Introduces sex therapist Larry James and discusses why women fake
orgasms.

Talking about Sex

content.health.msn.com/content/article/1/1700_50599
Links to the article "How Couples Can Communicate Their Needs
and Become More Sexually Adventurous" by sexologist Ava Cadell
from WebMD.

www.askmen.com/dating/curtsmith_60/msn_62c_dating_advice.html
Teaches individuals that communication is key and that variety is the
  spice of a relationship that may have become sexually boring.

www.mochasofa.com/family/program/expert/01december03a.asp
Enables couples to discuss their sexual concerns openly to improve
  their sex lives.

REFERENCES

Alvear, Michael. "Aging Disgracefully." *Frontiers Newsmagazine,* April 2001, 53.

Banks, Martha E., and Ellyn Kaschak. *Women with Visible and Invisible Disabilities: Multiple Intersections, Multiple Issues, Multiple Therapies.* Binghamton, N.Y.: Hayworth Press, 2003.

Basson, Rosemary. "The Female Sexual Response: A Different Model." *Journal of Sex and Marital Therapy* 26 (2000): 51–65.

———. "Report of the International Consensus Development Conference on Female Sexual Dysfunction: Definitions and Classifications." *The Journal of Urology* 163 (2000): 888–893.

Beier, K. M. "Differential Typology and Prognosis for Dis-sexual Behavior: A Follow-up Study of Previously Expert-Appraised Child Molesters." *International Journal of Legal Medicine* 111 (1998): 133–141.

Benson, Etienne. "The Science of Sexual Arousal." *Monitor on Psychology* 34, no. 4 (2003): 50–52.

Bingham, John E., and Chris Plotrowski. "On-Line Sexual Addiction: A Contemporary Enigma." *Psychological Reports* 79 (1996): 257–258.

Black, Donald W., Laura L. D. Kehrberg, Denise L. Flumerfelt, and Steven S. Schlosser. "Characteristics of 36 Subjects Reporting Compulsive Sexual Behavior." *American Journal of Psychiatry* 154, no. 2 (February 1997): 243–249.

Blanchard, Ray, Howard E. Barbaree, Anthony F. Bogaert, Robert Dickey, Philip Klassen, Michael E. Kuban, and Kenneth J. Zucker. "Fraternal Birth Order and Sexual Orientation in Pedophiles." *Archives of Sexual Behavior* 29, no. 5 (2000): 463–478.

Bridges, Michael R., John S. Wilson, and Carl B. Gacono. "A Rorschach Investigation of Defensiveness, Self Perception, Interpersonal Relations, and Affective States in Incarcerated

Pedophiles." *Journal of Personality Assessment* 70, no. 2 (1998): 365–385.

Bullard, David, and Susan Knight. *Sexuality and Physical Disability: Personal Perspectives.* St. Louis: C.V. Mosby, 1981.

Burns-Loeb, T., J. K. Williams, I. Rivkin, J. Vargas Carmona, G. Wyatt, D. Chin, and A. Asuan-O'Brien. "The Effects of Child Sexual Abuse on Adolescent and Adult Sexual Functioning." *The Annual Review of Sex Research,* in press.

Chan, A. O. M., L. E. C. Lim, and S. H. Ong. "A Review of Outrage of Modesty Offenders Remanded in a State Mental Hospital." *Medical Science and Law* 37, no. 4 (1997): 349–352.

Chin, D., G. E. Wyatt, J. Carmona, and T. Loeb. "Child Sexual Abuse and HIV: An Integrative Risk Reduction Approach." In *From Child Sexual Abuse to Adult Sexual Risk: Trauma, Revictimization and Intervention,* edited by L. Koenig, A. O'Leary, L. Doll, and W. Pequegnat. Washington, D.C.: American Psychological Association, in press.

Debusk, Robert. "Evaluating the Cardiovascular Tolerance for Sex." *American Journal of Cardiology* 86 (2000): 51–56.

Fackelmann, Kathleen. "Many of U.S. Kids Have Tried Huffing." *USA Today,* 14 March 2002, sec. 8D, p. 1.

Fernandez, Maria Elena. "Soul (Mate) Searching." *Los Angeles Times,* 17 June 2001, sec. E, p. 1–2.

Figueredo, Aurelio Jose, Bruce D. Sales, Kevin P. Russell, Judith V. Becker, and Meg Kaplan. "A Brunswikian Evolutionary-Developmental Theory of Adolescent Sex Offending." *Behavioral Science and the Law* 18 (2000): 309–329.

Francoeur, Robert T., Patricia B. Koch, and David L. Weis. *Sexuality in America.* New York: Continuum Publishing, 1999.

Gacono, Carl B., Meloy J. Reid, and Michael R. Bridges. "A Rorschach Comparison of Psychopaths, Sexual Homicide Perpetrators, and Nonviolent Pediophiles: Where Angels Fear to Tread." *Journal of Clinical Psychology* 56, no. 6 (2000): 757–777.

Harding, Richard, and Susan E. Golombok. "Test-Retest Reliability of the Measurement of Penile Dimensions in a Sample of Gay Men." *Archives of Sexual Behavior* 31, no. 4 (2002): 351–357.

Institute of Medicine. *Unequal Treatment: Confronting Racial and Ethnic Disparities in Health Care.* Washington, D.C.: National Academic Press, 2002.

Kafka, Martin. "Psycopharmacologic Treatments for Nonparaphilic Compulsive Sexual Behaviors." *CNS Spectrums* 5, no. 1 (2000): 49–59.

Kampert, Patrick. "For Cybercheats, the Affair Is Virtual but the Damage Is Real." *Los Angeles Times,* 3 February 2002, sec. E, p. 2.

Kelleher, Kathleen. "Birds and Bees." *Los Angeles Times,* 1 October 2001, sec. E, p. 1.

Kim, Peggy Y., and Michael Bailey. "Sidestreets on the Information Superhighway: Paraphilia and Sexual Variations on the Internet." *Journal of Sex Education and Therapy* 22, no. 1 (1997): 35–43.

Kinzl, Johann F., Christian Traweger, and Wilfried Biebl. "Sexual Dysfunctions: Relationship to Childhood Sexual Abuse and Early Family Experiences in a Nonclinical Sample." *Child Abuse and Neglect* 19, no. 7 (1995): 785–792.

Koch, Patricia B., and David L. Weis. *Sexuality in America: Understanding Our Sexuality Values and Behavior.* New York: Continuum, 1999.

Lamb, Michael. "Cybersex: Research Notes on the Characteristics of the Visitors to Online Chat Rooms." *Deviant Behavior: An Interdisciplinary Journal* 19 (1997): 121–135.

Langevin, R., S. Curnoe, and J. Bain. "A Study of Clerics Who Commit Sexual Offenses: Are They Different from Other Sex Offenders." *Child Abuse and Neglect* 24, no. 4 (2000): 535–545.

Langstrom, Niklas, Martin Grann, and Paul Lichtenstein. "Genetic and Environmental Influences on Problematic Masturbatory Behavior in Children: A Study of Same-Sex Twins." *Archives of Sexual Behavior* 31, no. 4 (2002): 343–350.

Laumann, Edward O., Anthony Pail, and Raymond C. Rosen. "Sexual Dysfunction in the United States: Prevalence and Predictors." *Journal of the American Medical Association* 281, no. 6 (1999): 537.

Lindsay, William R., Imelda Marshall, Clare Neilson, Kathleen Quinn, and Anne H. W. Smith. "The Treatment of Men with a Learning Disability Convicted of Exhibitionism." *Research in Development Disabilities* 19, no. 4 (1998): 295–316.

Meston, Cindy M., and Manuel Worcel. "The Effects of Yohimbine Plus L-arginine Glutamate on Sexual Arousal in Postmenopausal Women with Sexual Arousal Disorder." *Archives of Sexual Behavior* 31, no. 4 (2002): 323–332.

Murray, John B. "Psychological Profile of Pedophiles and Child Molesters." *Journal of Psychology* 134, no. 2 (2000): 211–224.

Plotnik, Rod, and Sandra Mollenauer. *Brain and Behavior.* New York: Harper & Row, 1978.

Rae, Stephen. "RX: Desire." *Modern Maturity* (March/April 2000): 88–94.

Rhynard, Jill, Marlene Krebs, and Julie Glover. "Sexual Assault in Dating Relationships." *Journal of Sexual Health* 67, no. 3 (1997): 89–93.

Ripique, Renee John R. "Assessment and Treatment of Persons with Pedophilia." *Journal of Psychosocial Nursing* 37, no. 12 (1999): 19–23.

Ross, Michael W., Ronny Tikkanen, and Sven-Axel Mansson. "Differences between Internet Samples and Conventional Samples of Men Who Have Sex with Men: Implications for Research and HIV Interventions." *Social Science and Medicine* 51 (2000): 749–758.

Ruzicka, Mary F. "Predictor Variables of Clergy Pedophiles." *Psychological Reports* 80 (1997): 589–590.

Sarwer, David B., and Joseph A. Durlak. "Childhood Sexual Abuse as a Predictor of Adult Female Sexual Dysfunction: A Study of Couples Seeking Sex Therapy." *Child Abuse and Neglect* 20, no. 10 (1996): 963–972.

Simpson, Grabame, Alex Blaszczynski, and Adeline Hodgkinson. "Sex Offending as a Psychosocial Sequela of Traumatic Brain Injury." *Journal of Head Trauma Rehabilitation* 14, no. 6 (1999): 567–580.

Smith, Deborah. "Women and Sex: What Is Dysfunction." *Monitor on Psychology* 34, no. 4 (2003): 54–56.

Stein, Dan J., and Donald W. Black. "Can Too Much Sex Be a Bad Thing?" *CNS Spectrums* 5, no. 1 (2000): 18.

Stein, Dan J. , Donald W. Black, and Willie Pienaar. "Sexual Disorders Not Otherwise Specified: Compulsive, Addictive or Impulsive." *CNS Spectrum* 5, no. 1 (2000): 60–64.

Stein, Dan J., Frans Hugo, Piet Oosthuizen, Susan M. Hawkridge, and Ben Van Heerden. "Neuropsychiatry of Hypersexuality." *CNS Spectrums* 5, no. 1 (2000): 36–48.

Sternberg, Steve. "The Danger of Living Down Low." USA Today, 15 March 2001, sec. D, pp. 1–2.

Stone, Howard T., William J. Winslade, and Craig M. Klugman. "Sex Offenders, Sentencing Laws and Pharmaceutical Treatment: A Prescription for Failure." *Behavioral Science and the Law* 18 (2000): 83-110.

Tanagho, Emil A., and Jack W. McAninch. *Smith's General Urology*. New York: Lange Medical Books/McGraw-Hill, 2000.

Tewksbury, Richard. "Patrons of Porn." *Deviant Behavior* 11 (1990): 259–271.

Warren, Janet I., Robert R. Hazelwood, and Park E. Dietz. "The Sexually Sadistic Killer." *Journal of Forensic Science* 41, no. 6 (1996): 970–974.

Waskul, Dennis, Mark Douglass, and Charles Edgley. "Cybersex: Outercourse and the Enselfment of the Body." *Symbolic Interaction* 23, no. 4 (2000): 375–397.

Weiss, Joseph. "Bondage Fantasies and Beating Fantasies." *Psychoanalytic Quarterly* 67 (1991): 626–644.

Wilson, Robin J. "Emotional Congruence in Sexual Offenders Against Children." *Sexual Abuse: A Journal of Research and Treatment* 11, no. 1 (1999): 33–46.

Wood, Raymond M., Linda S. Grossman, and Christopher G. Fichtner. "Psychological Assessment, Treatment, and Outcome with Sex Offenders." *Behavioral Science and the Law* 18 (2000): 23–41.

Wyatt, Gail E. *Stolen Women: Reclaiming Our Sexuality, Taking Back Our Lives*. New York: John Wiley and Sons, 1997.

About the Authors

Dr. Lewis Wyatt, Jr., is a licensed specialist in Obstetrics and Gynecology in California and Georgia. His distinguished career began after graduating from Meharry Medical College. He completed postgraduate studies at United States Public Health Service, the National Institute of Mental Health (NIMH), the University of Maryland, the University of Southern California, and the Kaiser Foundation Hospital in Los Angeles, California.

Dr. Wyatt's medical career has combined clinical, academic, and administrative practice. He has been recognized by his peers and elected chairman of the department of obstetrics and gynecology and subsequently chief of staff at Brotman Medical Center. He teaches residents at Cedars Sinai Medical Center in Los Angeles and has been involved in international grants funded by NIMH in Africa and India. Dr. Wyatt is the author or coauthor of several professional publications, and he speaks to medical professionals internationally. In 1992, he and his wife helped start Couples, the only organization for black married professionals that deals with relationships.

Gail Elizabeth Wyatt, Ph.D., was the first African American woman to become a licensed psychologist in the state of California. She is a sex therapist, Professor of Psychiatry and Biobehavioral Sciences, Director of the Sexual Health Program and Associate Director of both the AIDS Institute at UCLA and Drew Medical University. She earned her bachelor's and master's degrees at Fisk University and her doctorate and sex therapy training at UCLA. She externed at Meharry Medical

College and interned at the Neuropsychiatric Institute at UCLA. She is a fellow of five divisions of the American Psychological Association, a Diplomat of the American Board of Sexology, and a Fellow of the American Academy of Clinical Sexologists.

Dr. Wyatt has also devoted the past three decades of her career to understanding how sociocultural, gender, and relationship factors affect human sexuality and risks for sexually transmitted disease and HIV/AIDS transmission. She has been continuously funded by the National Institutes of Health, the California University–wide AIDS Program, or USAID since 1980. The author or a contributor to more than 100 professional publications and six books, she is also the editor-in-chief of *Cultural Diversity and Ethnic Minority Psychology*, the first journal of the American Psychological Association that focuses on the ethnicity and culture of diverse people. Her publications and books describing the sexuality of men, women, and adolescents are frequently cited in academic and popular media.

As a National Institute of Mental Health Research Scientist Career Development Awardee for seventeen years, Dr. Wyatt has conducted worldwide research that examines the consensual and abusive sexual relationships of men and women and the effects of these experiences on their psychological well-being. Her recent research includes a randomized clinical trial testing an eleven-week intervention for HIV-positive women with histories of early sexual abuse, as well as formative work with sexually abused African American and Latino men who have had sex with men but do not self-identify as gay and bisexual. In collaboration with colleagues at Columbia and Emory Universities, the University of Pennsylvania, and the NIMH, she is developing an intervention for HIV serodiscordant African American couples.

Dr. Wyatt was the first African American woman honored for distinguished contributions to research on public policy by the American Psychological Association. Her work has been recognized with many other honors and awards, among them the Dalmas Taylor Award for Leadership, Scholarship and Advocacy from the California State Psychological Association; the Carolyn Sherif Award from the Psychology of Women of the American Psychological Association; an honorary doctorate of letters from the California School of Professional Psychology; and the Silver Achievement Award from the Greater Los Angeles YWCA. As an alumnus, she is in the Dorsey High School (Los Angeles, Calif.) Hall of Fame. She has testified before the U.S. Congress eight times and has helped to strengthen laws and policy to protect the young and vulnerable from the effects of sexual abuse and other unwanted sexual outcomes.

Dr. Wyatt receives more speaking requests that she can accept, but makes time to mentor students worldwide, encouraging them to pursue careers in health and mental health professions. Her goal is to take what she has learned about conducting research within a cultural context and train the next generation of researchers and clinicians so that research and clinical care will reflect the reality and the strengths of diverse populations.

The Wyatts are the proud parents of two physicians, Dr. Lance E. Wyatt, a plastic surgeon, and Dr. Lacey Wyatt, a family practitioner. They have one granddaughter, Kamile, who brings them much joy.

INDEX

Stolen Women: Reclaiming Our Sexuality, Taking Back Our Lives

by Gail Wyatt

"Rich and empowering . . . the definitive account of black female sexuality."

—*Heart & Soul*

"*Stolen Women* gives us what Mama couldn't—a way to be in charge of our own bodies. This probing, fact-based book dissects the myths, discards the stereotypes, and unshackles our minds."

—Bebe Moore Campbell, author of *Brothers and Sisters*

"The culmination of twenty-two years of clinical practice and in-depth interviews with hundreds of African American women."

—*Ebony*

"Groundbreaking research breaks down why we came to be at increased risk and how we can protect ourselves for the future."

—*Essence*

"Finally, we have the first book that breaks the silence. Dr. Wyatt presents a well-researched and balanced perspective of the sexual experiences of African American women. It explodes the myths, examines our past, and sets the path for our healing and our future survival. This is a book that should be read by anyone who knows or cares about African American women."

—Gloria Johnson Powell, M.D.
Professor of Psychiatry,
Harvard University

"A long-awaited look at the stereotypes and sexual myths that surround African American women."

—*The Chicago Tribune*